# LINKING
## TEACHER EVALUATION
### and STUDENT LEARNING

Pamela D. Tucker & James H. Stronge

Association for Supervision and Curriculum Development
Alexandria, Virginia USA

Association for Supervision and Curriculum Development
1703 N. Beauregard St. • Alexandria, VA 22311-1714 USA
Phone: 800-933-2723 or 703-578-9600 • Fax: 703-575-5400
Web site: www.ascd.org • E-mail: member@ascd.org
Author guidelines: www.ascd.org/write

Gene R. Carter, *Executive Director;* Nancy Modrak, *Director of Publishing;* Julie Houtz, *Director of Book Editing & Production;* Tim Sniffin, *Project Manager;* Greer Beeken, *Graphic Designer;* Cynthia Stock, *Typesetter;* Tracey A. Franklin, *Production Manager*

Printed in the United States of America. Cover art copyright © 2005 by ASCD.
ASCD publications present a variety of viewpoints. The views expressed or implied in this book should not be interpreted as official positions of the Association.

The case study in Chapter 5 appears with permission of the Alexandria City Public Schools.

All Web links in this book are correct as of the publication date below but may have become inactive or otherwise modified since that time. If you notice a deactivated or changed link, please e-mail books@ascd.org with the words "Link Update" in the subject line. In your message, please specify the Web link, the book title, and the page number on which the link appears.

ASCD Member Book, No. FY05-6 (April 2005, PCR). ASCD Member Books mail to Premium (P), Comprehensive (C), and Regular (R) members on this schedule: Jan., PC; Feb., P; Apr., PCR; May, P; July, PC; Aug., P; Sept., PCR; Nov., PC; Dec., P.

Paperback ISBN: 1-4166-0032-9 • ASCD product #104136 • List Price: $26.95 ($20.95 ASCD member price, direct from ASCD only)
e-books ($26.95): retail PDF ISBN: 1-4166-0249-6 • netLibrary ISBN 1-4166-0247-X • ebrary ISBN 1-4166-0248-8

Quantity discounts for the paperback book: 10–49 copies, 10%; 50+ copies, 15%; for 500 or more copies, call 800-933-2723, ext. 5634, or 703-575-5634.

**Library of Congress Cataloging-in-Publication Data**

Tucker, Pamela D.
    Linking teacher evaluation and student learning / Pamela D. Tucker & James H. Stronge.
        p.  cm.
    Includes bibliographical references and index.
    ISBN 1-4166-0032-9 (alk. paper)
    1. Teachers—Rating of—United States—Case studies.  2. Teacher effectiveness—United States—Case studies.  3. Academic achievement—United States—Case studies.  I. Stronge, James H.  II. Title.

LB2838.T73  2005
371.14'4—dc22
                                                            2004026340

12  11  10  09  08  07  06  05          12  11  10  9  8  7  6  5  4  3  2  1

To the millions of children in our public schools whose futures are enhanced by the skills and efforts of highly capable and committed teachers and school leaders.

—Pamela D. Tucker and James H. Stronge

# LINKING
## TEACHER EVALUATION *and* STUDENT LEARNING

# Acknowledgments

Our convictions about the importance of using measures of student learning to assess teacher quality is based on years of working in and with many different public school systems that struggled to make teacher evaluation meaningful. We thank all of the teachers and administrators who have allowed us to be part of those conversations that have helped us to understand the concerns with current practice and the possibilities for better approaches.

An earlier version of this book was commissioned and published by the National Education Association (NEA). We wish to thank the NEA for granting the authors and ASCD permission to use portions of that book in this endeavor. In addition to earlier case studies, we have added one of the Alexandria, Virginia, City Schools, written by contributing authors Melissa McBride and Mason Miller.

During our data gathering for the book, we had the opportunity to talk with teachers, principals, central office administrators, and researchers in Colorado, Oregon, Tennessee, and Virginia. All of these individuals gave freely of their time, sometimes with great enthusiasm and sometimes with cautious concern, but always with the conviction of open-minded educators who wanted to improve education. Specifically, we'd like to express our appreciation to the researchers at the University of Tennessee Value-Added Research and Assessment Center; teachers and principals in the Knox

County Schools (Tennessee), and the Knox County Education Association; researchers at Western Oregon University's Teaching Research Division, and students in Western Oregon University's teacher preparation program; teachers and principals in the Alexandria City Public Schools (Virginia); and, finally, administrators and teachers in the Thompson R2J School District (Colorado). We wish to thank the wonderful central office administrators, evaluation specialists, principals, teachers, and researchers in each of these fine educational organizations that graciously opened their office and classroom doors to us and participated in our study. Your candor, support, and enthusiasm were refreshing.

Thanks also go to our graduate assistants, Melissa McBride, Michael Salmonowicz, and Jennifer Hindman, who provided invaluable assistance with background research for updating the case studies and extensive editorial assistance with the text.

We are grateful to Scott Willis at the Association for Supervision and Curriculum Development for his willingness to bring this information to a new audience with mounting expectations for instructional accountability. We hope that the ASCD audience will be receptive to the idea of more balanced teacher assessment based on both the *act* of teaching and the *results* of teaching.

Finally, we thank all of the readers who have been willing to make the paradigm shift in thinking about how to assess teacher quality.

# The Power of an Effective Teacher and Why We Should Assess It

*This is the value of the teacher, who looks at a face and says there's something behind that and I want to reach that person, I want to influence that person, I want to encourage that person, I want to enrich, I want to call out that person who is behind that face, behind that color, behind that language, behind that tradition, behind that culture. I believe you can do it. I know what was done for me.*

—Maya Angelou

The transformative power of an effective teacher is something almost all of us have experienced and understand on a personal level. If we were particularly fortunate, we had numerous exceptional teachers who made school an exciting and interesting place. Those teachers possessed a passion for the subjects that they taught and genuine care for the students with whom they worked. They inspired us to play with ideas, think deeply about the subject matter, take on more challenging work, and even pursue careers in a particular field of study. Some exceptional teachers achieve celebrity status, such as Jaime Escalante, the math teacher who inspired the film *Stand and Deliver,* but thousands of unsung heroes go unrecognized in their remarkable work with students on a daily basis.

## Qualities of Effective Teachers

We know intuitively that these highly effective teachers can have an enriching effect on the daily lives of children and their lifelong educational and career aspirations. We now know empirically that these effective teachers also have a direct influence in enhancing student learning. Years of research on teacher quality support the fact that effective teachers not only make students feel good about school and learning, but also that their work actually results in increased student achievement. Studies have substantiated that a whole range of personal and professional qualities are associated with higher levels of student achievement. For example, we know that verbal ability, content knowledge, pedagogical knowledge, certification status, ability to use a range of teaching strategies skillfully, and enthusiasm for the subject characterize more successful teachers.[1] The following are some of the key qualities of effective teachers:

- Have formal teacher preparation training.
- Hold certification of some kind (standard, alternative, or provisional) and are certified within their fields.
- Have taught for at least three years.
- Are caring, fair, and respectful.
- Hold high expectations for themselves and their students.
- Dedicate extra time to instructional preparation and reflection.
- Maximize instructional time via effective classroom management and organization.
- Enhance instruction by varying instructional strategies, activities, and assignments.
- Present content to students in a meaningful way that fosters understanding.
- Monitor students' learning by utilizing pre- and postassessments, providing timely and informative feedback, and reteaching material to students who did not achieve mastery.

• Demonstrate effectiveness with the full range of student abilities in their classrooms, regardless of the academic diversity of the students.

For a complete listing of these qualities with references, please refer to Appendix A.

Not only does a reasonable consensus exist on what effective teachers do to enhance student learning, but also meta-analyses by researchers such as Marzano, Pickering, and Pollock (2001) have begun to quantify the average effects of specific instructional strategies. When properly implemented, instructional strategies such as identifying similarities and differences, summarizing and note taking, and reinforcing effort and providing recognition can result in percentile gains of 29–45 points in student achievement.[2] Such an increase would mean that the score of an average student at the 50th percentile might rise to the 79th or even the 95th percentile with the effective use of selected instructional strategies. While teaching undeniably will remain an art, there is also a science to it that we are only beginning to aggressively apply to practice. As observed by Mike Schmoker, author of *Results: The Key to Continuous School Improvement*, "when we begin to more systematically close the gap between what we know and what we do, we will be on the cusp of one of the most exciting epochs in the history of education."[3] With state standards and federal legislation, such as No Child Left Behind, more explicitly defining accountability, the time has arrived for a systematic application of our research-based knowledge.

## Impact of Teacher Effectiveness on Student Achievement

The work of Bill Sanders, formerly at the University of Tennessee's Value-Added Research and Assessment Center, has been pivotal in reasserting the importance of the individual teacher on student learning.[4] One aspect of his research has been the additive or cumulative effect of teacher effectiveness on student achievement. Over a multi-year period, Sanders focused on what happened to students whose teachers produced high achievement versus those whose teachers produced low achievement results. He discovered that when children, beginning in 3rd grade, were placed with three high-performing teachers in a row, they scored on average at the 96th percentile on Tennessee's statewide mathematics assessment at the end of 5th grade.

When children with comparable achievement histories starting in 3rd grade were placed with three low-performing teachers in a row, their average score on the same mathematics assessment was at the 44th percentile,[5] an enormous 52-percentile point difference for children who presumably had comparable abilities and skills. Elaborating on this body of research, Dr. Sanders and colleagues reported the following:

> . . . the results of this study well document that the most important factor affecting student learning is the teacher. In addition, the results show wide variation in effectiveness among teachers. The immediate and clear implication of this finding is that seemingly more can be done to improve education by improving the effectiveness of teachers than by any other single factor. Effective teachers appear to be effective with students of all achievement levels, regardless of the level of heterogeneity in their classrooms.[6]

Further analysis of the Tennessee data indicated that the effects on achievement of both strong and weak teachers persisted over three years: subsequent achievement was enhanced or limited by the experiences in the classrooms of strong or weak teachers, respectively.[7] In other words, learning gains realized by students during a year in the classroom of an effective teacher were sustained over later years and were compounded by additional years with effective teachers. Conversely, depressed achievement results resisted improvement even after a student was placed with an effective teacher, and the negative impact was discernible statistically for approximately three subsequent years. Given results like these, it's no wonder that the researchers found that "a major conclusion is that teachers make a difference."[8]

In a comparable study by researchers in Dallas, Texas, similar results were found in both math and reading during the early grades.[9] When 1st grade students were fortunate enough to be placed with three high-performing teachers in a row, their average performance on the math section of the Iowa Tests of Basic Skills increased from the 63rd percentile to the 87th, in contrast to their peers with similar scores whose performance decreased from the 58th percentile to the 40th, a percentile difference of 42 points. A similar analysis in reading found a percentile difference of 44 percentile points. The studies in Tennessee and Texas produced strikingly similar findings: Highly effective teachers are able to produce much greater gains in student achievement than their less effective counterparts.

While the numbers help to summarize the cumulative academic effects of less effective teachers, we can only imagine the sense of failure and hopelessness that these children and their parents experienced during the years in these classrooms. Undoubtedly, the children wondered what was wrong with them when, in reality, it was the quality of their instruction. A common yet misguided bit of folk wisdom has been that adversity, in the guise of an ineffective teacher, builds character and that a student can catch up the following year. The research indicates otherwise.

Based on the findings from the Dallas Public Schools' Accountability System, the negative effects of a poor-performing teacher on student achievement persist through three years of high-performing teachers.[10] The good news is that if students have a high-performing teacher one year, they will enjoy the advantage of that good teaching in future years. Conversely, if students have a low-performing teacher, they simply will not outgrow the negative effects of lost learning opportunities for years to come. Further exacerbating the negative effects of poor-performing teachers, the Dallas research shows that "lower-achieving students are more likely to be put with lower effectiveness teachers . . . . Thus, the negative effects of less effective teachers are being visited on students who probably need the most help."[11]

Summarizing the findings from studies of the Dallas and Tennessee Value-Added Assessment Systems, Mendro states:

> Research . . . has demonstrated the effects of teachers on student achievement. They [the researchers] show that there are large additional components in the longitudinal effects of teachers, that these effects are much larger than expected, and that the least effective teachers have a long-term influence on student achievement that is not fully remediated for up to three years later.[12]

In straightforward terms, these residual effects studies make it clear that not only does teacher *quality* matter when it comes to how much students learn, but also that, for better or worse, a teacher's *effectiveness* stays with students for years to come.

## Highly Qualified Versus Highly Effective

Given the growing body of knowledge about the impact of effective teachers on children, it seems that educational policy is beginning to acknowledge the importance of classroom teachers in addition to curriculum standards and assessments. A case in point is the federal No Child Left Behind Act of 2001, which has introduced both the concepts of "adequate yearly progress," based on annual testing, and "highly qualified teacher," based on teacher credentials, as strategies to improve U.S. education. According to the legislation, "highly qualified" teachers are defined as those who hold at least a bachelor's degree, are fully licensed or certified by the state in the subjects they teach, and can demonstrate competence in the subjects they teach.

While licensure or certification is a significant indicator of teacher quality, these factors alone are insufficient for teacher effectiveness. As discussed earlier, teacher effectiveness is characterized by a far more complex set of qualities than one's professional preparation. It includes dispositions and an array of planning, organizational, instructional, and assessment skills. Effective teachers are able to envision instructional goals for their students, then draw upon their knowledge and training to help students achieve success. A "highly qualified" teacher is certainly a good starting point, but most of us would want our child to have a highly effective teacher whose teaching effort yields high rates of student learning.

## Promoting Teacher Effectiveness

How do we support and cultivate effective teachers for all our schools and all our children? It is our belief that teachers want and need feedback, not only on the *act* of teaching, but also on the *results* of teaching. Timely, informative feedback is vital to any improvement effort. For instance, consider the role of a track coach, fitness trainer, or weight counselor. These individuals provide guidance on *how* to perform better, but the evidence of their effectiveness as professionals manifests in tangible *results*: improved running time, weight lifted, or pounds lost. It is evident that "people work more effectively, efficiently, and persistently . . . while gauging their efforts against results."[13]

Teacher evaluation systems are often intended to serve the purpose of providing feedback and guidance for improving professional practice. In fact, most authors identify the fundamental purposes of teacher evaluation as improving performance and documenting accountability.[14] The *performance improvement function* relates to the personal growth dimension and involves helping teachers learn about, reflect on, and improve their practice. The improvement function generally is considered *formative* in nature and suggests the need for continuous professional growth and development.[15] The *accountability function*, on the other hand, reflects a commitment to the important professional goals of competence and quality performance. Accountability is typically viewed as *summative* and relates to judging the effectiveness of educational services.[16]

Teacher evaluation traditionally has been based on the *act* of teaching and documented almost exclusively through the use of classroom observations. In a study conducted by the Educational Research Service,[17] 99.8 percent of U.S. public school administrators used direct classroom observation as the primary data collection technique. However, primary reliance on formal observations in evaluation poses significant problems (e.g., artificiality, small sample of performance) for teacher evaluation.[18] Even under the best of circumstances, when principals might visit a classroom three or four times in a given year, the observation

- Can be artificial by nature,
- Suggests an inspection approach to supervision,
- Has limited validity based on the skill of the observer,
- Is narrow in scope (i.e., restricted to instructional skills only), and
- Involves a small sample of the teacher's actual work with students

(e.g., four hours of observation would equal less than 1/2 of 1 percent of a teacher's time teaching during a given year).[19]

Despite these substantial drawbacks to the traditional evaluation process, the truly fundamental flaw in such an approach is the assumption that the presence of good practice during the observation equates to the academic success of students. If student learning is our ultimate goal, then it should be measured directly and not extrapolated from limited observations of classroom instruction. A more balanced approach to teacher evaluation would involve an assessment of the *act* of teaching as well as the *results* of teaching. We don't suggest throwing out the use of classroom observation to foster teacher improvement; rather we advocate that teacher effectiveness be judged and demonstrated by both classroom instruction *and* the learning gains of students.

## Assessing Teacher Effectiveness

Most educators would agree that they are responsible for student learning, but the profession as a whole has avoided evaluations based on measures of student learning, sometimes with good reason, given the unfair approaches that have been proposed. The solution, however, is not to continue with traditional strategies simply because they are benign and comfortable, but rather to develop fair and reasonable means of assessing teacher success with students. A number of school systems and educational programs, to be discussed later in this book, have explored innovative ways of capturing valid and reliable data on student learning to inform the teacher evaluation process. Developing fair approaches for the assessment of teacher effectiveness requires an unflinching look at both the legitimate concerns that have driven the avoidance of a results orientation in the past, and the promising possibilities that make it more attractive in today's climate of greater accountability for student learning outcomes.

### Concerns

Concerns about assessing teacher quality based on measures of student learning have clustered around what Schalock[20] terms the collective and conditional nature of accountability, as well as the strategies for measuring student learning. Often, accountability efforts in schools are reduced to simplistic mandates for students to reach specified achievement goals at certain points in time. While gratifying as a bottom line, these expectations ignore the complex interdependencies of the learning enterprise. We must consider questions such as, "accountability by whom, with what resources, and as measured by what?"

**Collective nature of accountability: Responsibility by all stakeholders.** Accountability should be thought of as a collective responsibility for supporting learning by parents, principals, superintendents, school board members, *and* teachers, to say nothing of the students themselves. Holding teachers accountable for student achievement without recognition of the roles played by these other partners in the educational process is patently unfair and can amount to scapegoating. Likewise, requiring students to attend summer school, or retaining them due to limited progress, avoids the collective nature of accountability if school systems have not provided the quality of instruction necessary for students to meet grade level expectations.

Ultimately, learning is a phenomenon that occurs as a result of the interactions between a teacher and student. Teachers cannot be solely responsible for student learning because it is an internally controlled activity.

However, teachers are expected to optimize the conditions for learning. It is what they were hired to do and it is their professional obligation. As Schalock notes, "educator accountability for student progress in learning goes hand-in-hand with the social contract that assigns responsibility for education to schools."[21]

**Conditional nature of accountability: Resources and student needs.** Just as many actors affect the educational process, many variables affect the learning process within a classroom and are beyond the control of the individual teacher. These external variables include the level of support provided by the community and state, the availability of books for every child, the number of computers, sufficient instructional supplies, the support of curriculum specialists, and so forth. Within the classroom, the number and type of students can have dramatic effects on the level of academic achievement experienced by the class. Class size does make a difference, especially when a teacher is expected to work with a large number of at-risk students, whether they are disabled, limited in their English, or poor.

**Measurement of student learning.** One additional concern about the use of student learning assessments in the teacher evaluation process is the way in which learning is assessed. The traditional use of grades or standardized achievement scores is certainly suspect for a variety of reasons, including the

- Accuracy of grading procedures,
- Alignment of achievement tests with the curriculum,
- Diagnostic value of either approach for instructional improvement, and
- Single-point-in-time nature of these indicators.

In the absence of meaningful pre-test data, grades or achievement test scores at the end of the year are hardly valid measures of a teacher's influence during a given year; indeed, they reflect the cumulative effects of what students have learned at home and school over preceding years. A much more accurate measure of what a student has learned would be reflected by an assessment that is curriculum-aligned and administered both at the beginning and end of the year. When such learning gains are averaged over a whole class of students, we have a general indication of the magnitude of learning that took place with that group of children. (A more in-depth discussion of possible assessment strategies will be offered in Chapter 2.)

As has become evident, the interplay of factors affecting student learning is multifaceted and quite challenging. It is also difficult to reach consensus on how best to measure student learning. Given these complexities, many educators have avoided being too explicit or public about tracking student learning for the purpose of improving instruction or evaluating performance. However, the current context of high-stakes accountability for students and schools found in most states, and which is being developed as a result of No Child Left Behind, provides an impetus and urgency for examining ways to assess teacher quality that are fair and realistic. Today, superintendents, principals, teachers, and students are being held accountable for higher levels of student achievement. Teachers are being pressured to produce results, yet often lack the necessary information and support to make data-driven instructional decisions. The use of approaches such as those suggested in this book can offer feedback on how to improve instruction in a balanced and meaningful manner.

## Possibilities

Two primary purposes of teacher evaluation, as noted earlier, are professional growth and accountability. The use of data on student learning in the teacher evaluation process offers a potential tool for both improvement and for refocusing teacher evaluation on the accomplishments of teachers versus stylistic issues or their political standing. Too often, personal opinions or biases contaminate the evaluation process and undermine the credibility and trust necessary for meaningful dialogue about instruction. Reliable and valid information on student learning helps to align the evaluation process with the fundamental concerns of schooling. There are numerous advantages to this approach.

**More objective measure of teacher effectiveness.** The importance of objective data in the evaluation process becomes more striking in a story from one principal in Dallas. As she entered the new school to which she was assigned, the outgoing principal informed her of two problematic teachers for whom she would need to begin laying the groundwork to dismiss. One teacher tended to be scattered in her approach to tasks and had a somewhat disorganized room. Her students were often talking and moving around the room at will as they worked. The other teacher was brusque with her students, rigid with her class rules, and worked the students hard. They were polar opposites in terms of style, but at the end of the year, when the new principal received the test data on the teachers in her building, she found that both of these teachers were top performers in terms of gains in student achievement. She decided that she could tolerate individual personality differences if children were being well served by these teachers. This story offers a compelling message: an evaluation approach that examines both the *act* of teaching and the *results* of teaching provides a more balanced and realistic appraisal of teacher effectiveness.

**Meaningful feedback for instructional improvement.** Objective feedback in the form of assessment data also offers an invaluable tool for supervision. As Barbara Howard and Wendy McColskey note, "evaluation that leads to professional growth requires teachers to look honestly at their weaknesses and strengths."[22] Self-assessment can be limited because of a lack of objectivity. Feedback from colleagues or supervisors based on a few classroom visits is equally limited because of the narrow sampling of behavior it provides. Assessment data of student learning over a marking period or even half a year can provide substantive feedback on students' cumulative mastery of material. It provides a broader and richer sampling of the teacher's impact on students and permits the identification of specific patterns in the learning of content and skills that were taught.

The evidence from schools that have been successful in increasing the achievement level of students, particularly those serving high-poverty and high-minority populations, has been that better use of data is a key ingredient in their success.[23] Data analysis has been used as a means of monitoring success and ensuring accountability for the identified goals of schools and school systems. In a recent study of 32 schools in the San Francisco Bay area, the frequency with which teachers collected, interpreted, and analyzed data for instructional improvement was found to differ among schools that were closing the achievement gap versus those that were not. "Two-thirds of the teachers surveyed in the gap-closing schools said they used test and other data at least several times a month to understand their students' skills gaps, and sometimes several times a week."[24] Instructional responsiveness to student assessments is a powerful tool for increased student achievement.

**Barometer of success and motivational tool.** In addition to providing meaningful feedback for instructional improvement, student achievement data can provide encouragement and a sense of gratification. As Schmoker observes, "Data and results can be a powerful force for generating an intrinsic desire to improve."[25] Credible data on the results of teaching efforts inform instructors on what to change to improve their performance and gauge their success in doing so. Without concrete feedback on the results of their work, teachers can hardly hope to improve them. "Data make the invisible visible, revealing strengths and weaknesses that are easily concealed. Data promote certainty and precision, which increases teachers' confidence in their abilities."[26]

**Assessment is an integral facet of instruction.** More than 30 years ago, Lortie noted that "the monitoring of effective instruction is the heart of effective instruction."[27] Truly effective teachers monitor student learning on an ongoing basis and use the information to improve their teaching. How do we encourage all teachers to embrace this practice to benefit their teaching and the learning of their students? The purpose of *Linking Teacher Evaluation and Student Learning* is to present methodologies that have attempted to balance the competing demands of fairness, diagnostic value for professional growth, and accountability for student learning. The details of implementation are daunting; each methodology reflects years of careful consideration of the myriad issues that influence student learning and its assessment. All the models presented in this book have both advantages and disadvantages, but they have a proven track record for connecting teacher evaluation to student learning.

## Conclusion

Across the United States, school accountability is a theme now commonly heard in the regular discourse among state government officials and local community members. Parents, policymakers, and educators alike have examined their public schools and are calling for, even demanding, improvement. School reform efforts are taking a variety of forms, with two of the most prominent being a focus on higher teacher standards and improved student performance.

These goals were illuminated by the powerful opening salvo in the 1996 report, *What Matters Most: Teaching for America's Future*, by the National Commission on Teaching and America's Future, as follows:

We propose an audacious goal . . . by the year 2006, America will provide all students in the country with what should be their educational birthright: access to competent, caring, and qualified teachers.[28]

The commission followed this opening statement with its first of five major recommendations: *Get serious about standards for both students and teachers.* "Clearly, if students are to achieve high standards, we can expect no less from their teachers and other educators."[29]

If teachers do, in fact, make a difference in student learning, and if we are to have competent and caring teachers, shouldn't we relate teacher work to student work? Shouldn't student achievement be a fundamental measure of teacher effectiveness? We explore these questions in the remaining chapters. This introductory chapter is followed by an overview of the spectrum of strategies that have been developed to assess teacher effectiveness as a function of student learning. Then, in turn, we will examine four examples of assessment systems that rely on student learning as a measure of teacher effectiveness:[30]

1. Assessing Teacher Quality with Student Work: The Oregon Teacher Work Sample Methodology.

2. Assessing Teacher Quality in a Standards-Based Environment: The Thompson, Colorado, School District.

3. Assessing Teacher Quality Through Goal Setting: The Alexandria, Virginia, School District.

4. Assessing Teacher Quality Based on Student Gains: Value-Added Assessment in Tennessee.

The concluding chapter will summarize key issues and offer recommendations for educators and policy makers who are interested in making the connection explicit between teacher evaluation and student achievement.

# 2

# How Can We Assess
# Teacher Quality?

The processes of teaching and learning stimulate one another.
—Confucius

Given the central role that teachers have always played in successful schools, connecting teacher performance and student performance is a natural extension of the educational reform agenda. "The purpose of teaching is learning, and the purpose of schooling is to ensure that each new generation of students accumulates the knowledge and skills needed to meet the social, political, and economic demands of adulthood."[1] Thus, for many, it seems long overdue to ensure that student learning gains are taken into account in the design and implementation of teacher assessment systems. In this chapter, we provide a brief overview of four teacher assessment models that do, in fact, include student performance as a fundamental part of their overall assessment of teacher effectiveness and quality:

1. The Oregon Teacher Work Sample Methodology.
2. The Thompson, Colorado, School District Standards-Based Assessment System.

3. The Alexandria, Virginia, School District Goal-Setting System.
4. The Tennessee Value-Added Assessment System.

But first, we turn our attention to these questions:

- Are teachers responsible for student learning?
- What are the options for assessing student learning?

## Are Teachers Responsible for Student Learning?

The argument can be made that student learning is both the responsibility and choice of the individual student. Consider the following quote, which espouses this position:

> Because every person is accountable for his or her own behavior but not for what other people do, teachers must be held accountable for what they do as teachers but not for what their students do as learners. Students are responsible for their own learning.[2]

Ultimately, this position is quite accurate. As Elliot Eisner acknowledges, it is the students who must integrate and make sense of new knowledge or practice new skills.[3] Without their participation, it is possible that no learning will take place. In fact, in many states, high-stakes testing programs are holding students responsible for their learning by denying promotion, requiring summer school, and delaying graduation. But is learning solely the responsibility of students?

Most of us would agree that learning is a partnership between teachers and students in which both hold responsibility. Indeed, many educators believe that teaching has not taken place if students have not learned. Research clearly suggests that teachers and the quality of their instruction directly affect student learning. If teachers can influence learning, then is it not a professional obligation to promote the greatest amount of learning possible? As noted in the report of the National Commission on Teaching & America's Future, "A caring, competent, and qualified teacher for every child is the most important ingredient in education reform and, we believe, the most frequently overlooked."[4]

The process-product research summarized by Brophy and Good[5] and a host of others has supported the positive effects of certain teaching practices that enhance student achievement gains. Clearly, teachers are the school's primary point of contact with students and in large part determine the outcomes of educational goals and learning results for students.[6] A substantial body of research has supported the broader contention that teacher quality—as defined in numerous ways—directly affects student learning.[7] In a sweeping meta-analysis of available studies on what variables impact school learning, Wang, Haertel, and Walberg found a "general agreement among experts" regarding these influences.[8] One of their major conclusions was that distal variables such as state, district, and even school-level policy have little direct influence on school learning; it is variables like psychological factors, instructional characteristics, and home environment that have more impact. Schools obviously have the greatest control over instructional characteristics as determined by classroom teachers.[9]

Given this research base, we believe that teachers are responsible not only for teaching but also, to some extent, for learning outcomes. If this position is accepted, then there is the question of how to measure learning outcomes.

## The Evolution of Student Learning Assessments

Over the centuries, educators have employed various strategies to evaluate their students' learning. In many respects, the evaluation measures selected were reflective of the society within which they existed. In the days of Plato, students demonstrated their knowledge and understanding via oral examinations.[10] During the Protestant Reformation, students were assessed upon their abilities to memorize and deliver portions of religious texts. Shaped by these European traditions, memorization and recitation of specific passages or catechisms continued to be the primary measure of student learning in Colonial America.[11] After the Revolutionary War and into the early 20th century, the content delivered to students in the United States was more secular in nature and reflected the ideals of democracy; however, oral examinations continued as the main assessment strategy.[12] After the post-Civil War reconstruction era, the United States experienced a period of industrial modernization characterized by mass production.[13] With the increased availability of paper and the invention of the steel pen in the latter portion of the 19th century, written exams began to take hold as the primary means to appraise a student's knowledge.[14]

The dawn of the 20th century brought with it the mass distribution of lead pencils and a new breed of assessment, the standardized achievement test.[15] Psychologists such as Thorndike and Terman sought to design uniform assessments "to evaluate the inherent abilities of students in order to make decisions about the kind of educational opportunities they should have."[16] Today, standardized testing has become a political reality in the mandated programs that exist in almost every state. The fundamental question, however, that should drive educational policy and practice in the testing debate is simple: Do tests improve student learning? All other reasons, such as accountability, teacher evaluation, and program evaluation, cannot be justified unless they somehow enhance student learning. The loss of instructional time, restricted curriculum scope, the anxiety testing creates, the sense of failure some students and schools experience, and the unjustified conclusions that are drawn from test scores all argue against the use of tests unless they can be put to a compelling purpose.[17] Given the grave, unintended consequences of high-stakes testing, tests must be used with great care and concern for those involved in the enterprise and with the goal of better educational outcomes for students.

Despite the concerns and criticisms that often are leveled at today's high-stakes testing, it is a reality. Furthermore, growing evidence suggests that the impact of high-stakes testing can produce positive results. For instance, a study in Chicago on student achievement in promotional gate grades found that test scores increased substantially following the introduction of high-stakes testing. More specifically, in reading, "students with low skills experienced the largest improvement in learning gains in the year prior to testing, while students with skills closer to their grade level experienced the greatest benefits in mathematics."[18] In another study, this time on the impact of high-stakes testing on the National Assessment of Education Progress (NAEP) mathematics test from 1996–2000, the researchers found that "students in high-accountability states averaged significantly greater gains on the NAEP 8th-grade math test than students in states with little or no state measures to improve student performance."[19]

The critical role played by testing takes on particular urgency when it indicates the mastery of basic skills such as reading, writing, and computing.

Without these skills, elementary students are truly doomed to failure. Therefore, we must identify these skill deficits early and address them aggressively if we are to provide the foundation for all later learning. No amount of ingenious teaching can compensate for the lack of instructional level reading skills in the later grades. Poor reading skills compromise possible achievement throughout a student's school career. Tests are one means of ensuring a minimum standard of quality, especially for children who are in the poorest schools, by illuminating the vast discrepancies in student achievement levels.

Fortunately, student learning can and should be demonstrated by a variety of assessments. The range of possible strategies to assess student learning includes

- Norm-referenced achievement tests,
- Criterion-referenced tests, and
- Other types of student assessments.

## Norm-Referenced Achievement Tests

The standardized tests widely used in schools are "multiple-skill achievement tests that evaluate knowledge and understanding in several curricular areas."[20] Typically they are group-administered and norm-referenced, providing comparisons to other students in the same grade level across the country. Considerations in selecting an achievement test or test battery include content validity (e.g., proper match between the test and the subject matter taught), the test ceiling (e.g., the test should not be too easy for the students), and related issues. Questions that norm-referenced tests typically answer include:

- Where does a student stand in a given area of achievement in relation to other students and compared to the norm group of students?
- How does the overall achievement in one teacher's class compare with that of another's?
- How does the achievement in the given content area for students in the selected school district compare with the national norms or with another school district?[21]

See Appendix B for examples of norm-referenced tests.

### Criterion-Referenced Tests

Criterion-referenced measurement is "an approach to assessment in which a student's test performance is interpreted according to how much of a defined assessment domain has been mastered by the student."[22] Typically, they are designed to test whether students have reached an established criterion in a clearly defined domain. Questions that criterion-referenced tests answer include:

- What is a student's level of knowledge in the domain (e.g., what percentage of problems of a given type can we expect the student to solve correctly)?
- What are the student's specific strengths and deficiencies in the domain?
- What are the specific strengths and weaknesses of a given school program or curriculum?
- What specific changes in student performance have occurred as a result of changing the curriculum or instruction?[23]

See Appendix B for examples of criterion-referenced tests.

While standardized tests, both norm-referenced and criterion-referenced, are insufficient to judge the whole of student learning (and certainly not teacher effectiveness), they can provide information on various dimensions of learning, such as the acquisition of basic knowledge and skills. The information tests provide seems to be a good starting point for identifying students who have difficulty learning material or teachers who have difficulty teaching specific content. Diagnosing the precise problem and providing the needed assistance require professional understanding of the dynamics of teaching and learning. Standardized testing should not be used as a final judgment of failure or success, but as an indicator or source of information about possible problems that educators can analyze systematically for patterns of strength and weakness.

### Other Types of Student Assessments

Additional types of frequently used student assessments include authentic measures of student performance and locally-developed assessments. Examples of authentic assessments include writing samples, student portfolio entries, and other performance-based assessments. Examples of locally-developed assessments include teacher-made tests, grade level or department (e.g., math) tests, and district-wide assessments. See Appendix B for more examples of other types of student assessments.

These assessments can easily be used in conjunction with one another. For example, performance assessment is a "practice that requires students to create evidence through performance that will enable assessors to make valid judgments about 'what they know and can do' in situations that matter."[24] Eisner suggests the possibility that both standardized tests and performance assessments could be used with students to focus on both their general skills and particular talents. The former would provide comparative data; the latter, individualized reflections of student learning. Each would complement the other by offering a different perspective of the student and acknowledging the competing demands of assessments in public education.

## How Can Teacher Assessment and Student Learning Be Connected?

A number of school systems and states have begun the process of linking student learning to the evaluation of teachers. Methodologies vary widely from highly systemic approaches to more individually tailored ones. In this section, we will profile four accountability systems that link student assessment and teacher evaluation. Each system has unique features that were developed to enhance the fairness of the assessment strategies for measuring student learning and using the results for teacher evaluation (Figure 2.1). They span a continuum from the more qualitative approach found in the Oregon Work Sample Methodology to the highly empirical approach used in Tennessee. They also vary in terms of the types of measures used to assess student learning. While each evaluation system will be presented in detail in Chapters 3–6, here we introduce the distinguishing features of each.[25]

### Assessment Through Student Work:
### The Oregon Teacher Work Sample Methodology
The ambitious goal of the Oregon Teacher Work Sample Methodology (TWSM) is to find better ways to assess the complexities of teaching and its

connections to student learning. "TWSM has been designed to portray the learning progress of pupils *on outcomes desired by a teacher* and taught by a teacher over a sufficiently long period of time for appreciable progress in learning to occur."[26] Consequently, TWSM requires that teachers document an extended sample of their work that includes

- Descriptions of the context of the teaching and learning,
- Desired learning outcomes,
- Instructional plans and resources,
- Assessments used, and, finally,
- The growth in learning achieved by students.

Further, the process requires teachers to reflect on their own teaching and its effects in terms of the learning achieved by each of their students.

## Assessment in a Standards-Based Approach:
## The Thompson, Colorado, School District

The teacher assessment program of Colorado's Thompson School District is a straightforward, easy-to-understand teacher assessment system. The standards-based evaluation system uses student achievement as only one factor in the teacher's performance review. Benchmarks for student learning goals are set with both standardized tests and informal assessments used to measure performance. Student achievement is measured using pre- and postinstruction measures that are selected based on content standards. When the time comes for an annual evaluation conference between the teacher and the principal, the teacher submits evidence of student learning based on gain scores, which is reviewed as part of the evaluation cycle. Results of the evaluation cycle are then connected to the teacher's professional growth plan for the following year. Thus, improvement in teacher performance is the hallmark of the system.

## Assessment Through Goal-Setting:
## The Alexandria, Virginia, School District

Alexandria City Public School System's Performance Evaluation Program (PEP) is a comprehensive evaluation system designed to portray the complex

**FIGURE 2.1**
**Key Features of Each Teacher Assessment System**

| Practice | Oregon: Work Sample Methodology Model | Thompson School District (Colo.): Standards-Based Model | Alexandria School District (Va.): Student Academic Goal-Setting Model | Tennessee: Value-Added Assessment System |
|---|---|---|---|---|
| What is the basis for the system? | Student growth is measured with pre- and postinstruction measures that are context-specific and selected based on desired outcomes. | Benchmarks for student learning goals are set with standardized tests and informal assessments and are used pre- and postinstruction to measure performance. | Teacher performance is assessed through: (1) the teacher's performance on established job standards, and (2) evidence of student achievement through annual pre- and postassessment of student progress. | Student growth on assessment measures is compared to each student's own previous growth rate and compiled at the classroom, school, and district level. |
| What are the student assessment measures? | The TWSM relies on authentic classroom assessments to document student learning. | • Colorado State Assessment Program: 3rd–10th grades.<br>• Criterion-referenced tests.<br>• Classroom assessments. | Student assessment varies depending on the grade and assignment of the teacher, and includes:<br>• Virginia Standards of Learning standards-based assessments.<br>• Criterion-referenced tests.<br>• Classroom assessments.<br>• Norm-referenced tests. | • Tennessee Comprehensive Assessment Program (every year: grades 3–8).<br>• End-of-course tests in high school.<br>• Writing assessment. |

| | | | | |
|---|---|---|---|---|
| How does the system work? | The Oregon TWSM employs a gain score measure to calculate student learning. | Evidence of student learning based on gain scores is submitted and reviewed as part of the evaluation process. | Student achievement goal-setting includes:<br>• Establishing benchmark performance data for each student.<br>• Determining instructional strategies to focus on the needs of each student.<br>• Assessing at the end of the academic course or year to determine student academic growth. | Statistical analysis of the data is used to generate<br>• School system reports.<br>• School-level reports.<br>• Individual teacher reports.<br>Test results are one source but cannot be the sole source of information for a broader evaluation process. |
| What are the goals of the system? | The TWSM is designed to foster both formative and summative teacher reflection and self-evaluation. | Teacher performance improvement is emphasized. The results of the evaluation cycle are connected to professional development in the upcoming evaluation cycle. | Goal-setting is intended to improve quality and effectiveness of instruction via professional development in order to improve student learning. | Professional development of teachers focuses on enhancing student learning. Focus is on student growth. |

*Source:* Reprinted with permission from Hindman, J., Stronge, J., and Tucker, P. (2003) Raising the bar: *Virginia Journal of Education, 97*(3), 6–10

nature of teaching. The evaluation system consists of four main components: formal observations, informal observations, portfolios, and academic goal-setting. The fourth component, academic goal-setting, seeks to link teacher instruction to student achievement by requiring teachers to set annual quantifiable goals related to their students' academic progress. As a value-added student growth model, student goal-setting can be customized for each class and teacher depending on instructional goals. The process places emphasis on professional development and improved student achievement. To determine which academic goals to set, teachers use the following guidelines:

- Identifying the content area to be addressed.
- Collecting baseline data for student performance using the best available means.
- Establishing student performance goals based on the baseline data.
- Determining instructional strategies for meeting the student performance goals.
- Providing instruction based on the strategies.
- Assessing student performance at the end of the course or year.
- Measuring student progress by comparing end results with baseline data.

## Assessment Based on Student Gains:
## Value-Added Assessment in Tennessee

The Tennessee Value-Added Assessment System (TVAAS) was developed by William Sanders using a statistical model based on growth or gains in student achievement scores rather than fixed standards. The Tennessee Comprehensive Assessment Program provides yearly measures of student learning in grades 2–8. Based on this rich source of data, the TVAAS compares each individual student's growth to his or her own previous growth rate. That is, this year's gains for each individual student are compared to the gains made in previous years. With TVAAS, all students serve as their own control for learning gains; it is assumed that the same potential for learning exists each year. Average student gains are calculated at the teacher level to determine if expected student learning was achieved. This information is then used to assist in the development of professional growth plans by teachers.

### Comparing the Four Teacher Assessment Approaches

All four of the teacher evaluation approaches emphasize using pre- and postmeasures of student learning to assess improvement or gains. The approaches to measuring student achievement vary from teacher-developed to standardized tests, but in every case, data are used as only one of multiple measures of teacher effectiveness. The student achievement information is used primarily for the purpose of better focusing instruction and fostering professional development. Figure 2.1 provides a summary of their respective distinguishing characteristics.

# Conclusion

Teacher evaluation is a major component of the educational agenda today. Although observation and evaluation of teachers have traditionally represented a major responsibility of principals and other supervisors, these functions have become even more significant in today's era of accountability. Clearly, paying closer attention to teaching practices and their effects on student learning has become standard practice in an effort to improve the quality of teaching and learning. In addition, teachers today are encouraged to take major responsibility for their own professional development. In an ideal situation, teachers and their supervisors work together to develop an evaluation system that (1) supports continued professional growth and (2) ensures accountability for the school and the school system. More systematically organized information on student learning can support both goals as well as enhance the evaluation process.

# 3

# Assessing Teacher Quality with Student Work: The Oregon Teacher Work Sample Methodology

A child miseducated is a child lost.

—John F. Kennedy

The ambitious goal of the Oregon Teacher Work Sample Methodology (TWSM) is to find better ways to assess the complexities of teaching and its connections to student learning. We selected TWSM to review as one model for teacher assessment because of its potential to provide systematic ways and means of assessing real samples of teacher work and the resulting work of students. Another key reason for featuring the Oregon teacher work sample approach is its applicability for prospective and new teachers.

## What Are the Purposes of the Assessment System and How Was It Developed?

The TWSM process is designed to foster formative and summative teacher reflection and self-evaluation, both of which are "important components of teachers' professional development. It focuses teachers on pupil learning as

26

the fundamental purpose and criterion of good teaching."[1] In alluding to the important relationship between teaching and the resulting learning, Del Schalock, one of the key developers of the methodology, stated that "the underpinning of medicine is healing, not the methods the physicians use."[2] The focus for improvement and accountability in this medical analogy is on what happens as a result of the intervention, and far less on the process of the intervention itself. Likewise, as reflected in the TWSM, the explicit purpose of teaching and, consequently, teacher evaluation is to focus on the impact of teaching and provide a direct link between teaching and learning. Simply put, TWSM is built upon the "assumption that the job of teaching is 'are kids making progress?'"[3]

The TWSM is an outgrowth of educational reform in Oregon, whose legislature passed an educational reform statute in 1991 that required schooling to be "extensively restructured so that all students would meet high standards."[4] Consistent with this legislative mandate, the Oregon Teacher Standards and Practices Commission instituted a redesign of teacher licensure requirements to reflect a standards-based model of schooling. As a result, an appraisal method was "developed that is meaningful to emerging teachers . . . and grounded in the complex reality of what teachers do. This appraisal method has come to be known as *teacher work sample methodology*."[5]

The vast majority of the TWSM development to date has been with pre-service teachers, and has been used to assess their teaching competencies as part of initial teacher licensure. Nonetheless, the TWSM approach is similar to many teacher evaluation systems that include portfolios or other samples of teacher work. Kenneth Wolf and colleagues describe teaching portfolios as "increasingly popular tools for both evaluation and professional development," due in part to their authentic nature.[6] Likewise, the developers and researchers of the Oregon TWSM refer to this assessment process as "close to a teacher's work"[7]:

> When complete, a teacher's work sample can be viewed as a compact, delimited teacher portfolio, with some important differences . . . For example, a portfolio typically represents a fairly long span of time (e.g., an entire school year, with supporting materials from previous years, whereas a teacher work sample brings a fine focus to a shorter period of teaching and learning). More important, whereas a teacher portfolio can include a broad representation of a teacher's work and professional development, TWSM is designed to focus teachers on [selected] issues . . . .[8]

The goal of the Teacher Effectiveness Project at Western Oregon University is to create:

> . . . a fully developed, validated, and reliable TWSM that provides a conceptual framework with which teachers and teacher development programs (preservice and in-service) can think about, learn about, practice, and demonstrate their proficiencies along a number of dimensions related to schools. TWSM is a methodology designed to serve training and research functions, as well as evaluation and licensure functions.[9]

Given the intent to develop TWSM as a reliable and valid teacher assessment approach that is appropriate for multiple purposes, including formative and summative evaluation, we will briefly examine the evidence related to these technical attributes. Then, we will review *how* the TWSM system works.

## Reliability Evidence

A key question to be answered is, does the methodology produce consistent results? The developers were aware that work sample products and performance must be judged consistently across raters. In their efforts to answer this thorny question, the developers checked for levels of agreement between college and school supervisor ratings provided around a student teacher's work sample implementation (performance in the classroom). The findings of this study were encouraging, with inter-rater agreement ranging from 81–98 percent.[10]

## Validity Evidence

The developers considered various forms of validation evidence (the degree to which the TWSM measures what it purports to measure) with the results reported in Figure 3.1.[11] In summarizing the technical development of the TWSM, the developers noted the following:

> Content (face) and construct validity do not appear to be a problem for most of the measures obtained through TWSM *so long as one does not wish to draw inferences about performance or effectiveness of a teacher beyond the sample of teaching and learning represented in a particular sample of work.* If one wishes to make such inferences, and there is a strong tendency to do so, then the technical issues involved become as much a matter of ensuring an adequate sample of teaching contexts and learning outcomes pursued as they do of ensuring the adequacy of measures used.[12]

---

**FIGURE 3.1**
**Teacher Work Sample Methodology Validation Evidence**

| Type of Validation | Evidence Gathered by Developers |
|---|---|
| • *Face validity:* the appearance, relevance, and clarity of the scoring guides used to rate performance and product quality with TWSM. | Feedback from teacher focus groups indicated that they generally viewed the TWSM as reasonable and reflective of "what teachers do." Thus, on its face, the process appears to be reasonable. |
| • *Content validity:* the degree to which the TWSM aligns with descriptions of what teachers do and the domains of effective teacher knowledge and skills. | Analyses were conducted to compare the proficiencies measures by the TWSM with other accepted frameworks of what effective teaching involves. The results of these comparative analyses yielded good matches with various frameworks, including Scriven's *Duties of The Teacher (DOTT),*[*] Educational Testing Service,[**] and the National Board for Professional Teaching Standards.[†] |
| • *Construct validity:* the degree to which the TWSM aligns with the philosophy of teaching and learning embodied in the policies of the state's teacher licensing agency and, more broadly, with the state's design for schooling.[††] | The TWSM is designed to maintain a focus on student learning as the central purpose and outcome of teaching. In an effort to measure this desired teaching-learning connection, regression analyses conducted (using teacher-reported student learning measures) indicated that teacher work sample measures accounted for between 24.5 percent (grades 3–5) and 59.5 percent (grades 6–8) of the variance observed in student learning. These data suggest that what teachers do has a measurable influence on student learning. |

[*] Scriven, M. (1994). Duties of the teacher. *Journal of Personnel Evaluation in Education, 8,* 151–184.
[**] Danielson, C. (1996). *Enhancing professional practice: A framework for teaching.* Alexandria, VA: Association for Supervision and Curriculum Development.
[†] National Board for Professional Teaching Standards. (1989). *Toward high and rigorous standards for the teaching profession.* Washington, DC: Author.
[††] While appropriate for the intended purpose of comparing the TWSM with Oregon's teacher licensure requirements, this definition of construct validity is narrower than would be desired for the use of TWSM to evaluate practicing teachers.

*Source:* Reprinted with permission of Western Oregon University.

Although the validation evidence for TWSM is encouraging, it is important to note that predictive validity (the degree to which results generated through the TWSM can forecast the effectiveness of practicing teachers) has yet to be established.[13] Thus, although the methodology is promising, its application needs to be validated with evidence that it can accurately differentiate future performance.

## How Does the Assessment System Work?

The Oregon Teacher Work Sample Methodology is anchored in an "outcome-based and context-dependent" theory of teacher effectiveness.[14] Its design requires teachers and their evaluators to identify and align the following issues:

- What are the learning outcomes I want *my* students to accomplish?
- What activities and instructional methodologies are appropriate or necessary for *these* students to achieve *these* outcomes?
- What resources and how much time do I need to implement these activities or methodologies?
- What assessment activities or methodologies are appropriate for these students and these outcomes when using these instructional methodologies?
- How successful was I at helping my students achieve the outcomes desired?
- What went right? What went wrong? Why?[15]

### Implementation Procedures

"As an approach to measurement, TWSM has been designed to portray the learning progress of pupils *on outcomes desired by a teacher and taught by a teacher* over a sufficiently long period of time for appreciable progress in learning to occur."[16] Consequently, the TWSM requires that teachers document an extended sample of their work. The work sample must include descriptions of the teaching and learning context, learning outcomes to be addressed, instructional plans and resources, assessments used, and the growth in learning achieved by students on targeted outcomes. Further, the process requires teachers (and prospective teachers) "to assess and reflect on their own performance in terms of the learning achieved by each of their students . . . ."[17] Thus, a vital aspect of the TWSM is intended to go beyond the teaching-learning processes and products; it is designed to encourage, even require, significant *reflection* on the work as the professional continuously attempts to improve the art and science of teaching.

"Simply put, TWSM requires teachers to think about, develop, implement, document, and present samples of their work as evidence of their effectiveness."[18] A central feature of this process is documenting evidence of student progress in learning. As an authentic and applied teacher performance appraisal measure, teachers are asked to implement the following nine steps:

1. Define the sample of teaching and learning to be described.

2. Identify learning outcomes to be accomplished within the work to be sampled.

3. Assess the learning status of students prior to instruction with respect to the postinstructional outcomes.

4. Align instruction and assessment with outcomes to be accomplished.

5. Describe the context in which teaching and learning are to occur.

6. Adapt outcomes desired, and related plans for instruction and assessment, to accommodate the demands of the teaching-learning context.

7. Implement a developmentally and contextually appropriate instructional plan.

8. *Assess the postinstructional accomplishments of learners and calculate on a student-by-student basis the growth in learning achieved.*

9. Summarize, interpret, and reflect on student learning growth and other assessment information.

Step 8 is italicized "to emphasize that.TWSM makes explicit to all constituencies the inclusion and prominence of students' learning gains in the definition of 'teacher effectiveness.'"[19]

## Formula for Calculating Student Learning Gains

The TWSM model employs a gain score measure to calculate student learning and to infer the teacher's influence on the learning. Beginning with pretest scores for all students in a classroom, the teacher first calculates a *percentage correct* score for each student. Then, the teacher

1. Tabulates the range of pre-instructional scores,
2. Sorts the scores into high-, middle-, and low-scoring groups, and
3. Calculates the mean scores for each of the groups as well as for the

class as a whole.

Using these pre-instructional data as a baseline, the teacher can then establish a level of standardization of the selected teacher-designed and curriculum-aligned measures of pupil learning. Calculating an Index of Pupil Growth (IPG) score for each pupil achieves this. The IPG is a simple metric devised by Jason Millman[20] to show the percentage of potential growth each pupil actually achieved. The metric is calculated as follows:

$$\frac{\text{(Postpercent correct)} - \text{(Prepercent correct)}}{\text{(100 percent} - \text{Prepercent correct)}}$$

Multiplying this metric by 100 results in a score that can range from −100 to +100. A negative number represents a lower score on the post-test than on the pre-test, a positive number represents a higher score on the post-test, and a score of +100 represents a perfect score on the post-test regardless of pre-test performance. A negative score is rare, with most scores falling within the +30 to +80 range.[21]

## Illustration of How the TWSM Works

How are these concepts and the scoring rubric applied in the assessment of a teacher's work? Figure 3.2 provides the key components drawn from an actual elementary school life science work sample that might serve to illustrate this process.[22]

## Only One of Multiple Measures

The TWSM is a highly structured and fairly complex assessment process. Nonetheless, it is viewed as only one among several information sources to be used in making judgments about teacher effectiveness. "Teacher work sample methodology is an extended applied performance assessment comprising multiple performance tasks. For prospective teachers . . . the results of this assessment are used as one source of evidence in gauging their

**FIGURE 3.2**
**Elementary Life Science "Spiders" Work Sample**

| Key Components in Work Sample | Details Provided |
|---|---|
| Background information | • Description of the school and classroom<br>• Student demographic information |
| Lesson outline | • Rationale for the lesson unit<br>• Learning goals and objectives<br>• Graphic organizer for the lesson sequence<br>• Lesson plan details (e.g., materials, instructional sequence, time estimate)<br>• Materials to be used in the lesson |
| Student assessment plan | • Pre- and postassessment procedures<br>• Instruction and assessment alignment matrix<br>• Scoring guide for student work |
| Work sample assessment results | • Samples of student work<br>• Net learning gains (postassessment – pre-assessment = learning gains) by individual students<br>• Net learning gains by student groups in clusters |
| Teacher reflection | • Assessment analysis—narrative summary and review of student learning results<br>• Reflective essay—narrative discussion of what went right, what went wrong, and how to improve in future lessons |

*Source:* Reprinted with permission of Western Oregon University.

attainment of teaching proficiencies at specified benchmarks . . . ."[23] The successful completion of at least two teacher work samples and their related assessment is required for initial licensure in Oregon. As with all other teacher evaluation systems we consider in this book, multiple measures of performance (including standardized measures such as the California Test of Basic Skills and the Praxis assessment series) are required.

Figure 3.3 summarizes key processes and protocols that the Oregon TWSM uses. The methodologies for the model and work sample are provided in Appendix C.

**FIGURE 3.3**
**List of Teacher Work Sample Methodology Descriptions and Guidelines**

| Protocol | Description |
|---|---|
| TWSM Product and Process Model | This graphic provides a model that summarizes key steps in the Teacher Work Sample Methodology. |
| Work Sample Methodology | This document provides a detailed description for creating a standards-based curriculum design using the TWSM. |
| Work Sample Scoring Scale | The scoring scale provides descriptors for six performance levels for a work sample. |

*Source:* Reprinted with permission of Western Oregon University.

## What Are the Advantages and Disadvantages of the Assessment System?

In our effort to discern strengths and weaknesses of the Oregon TWSM, we reviewed research findings published by the TWSM development team as well as critiques of the process by noted educational researchers with an interest in teacher assessment.[24] We also interviewed program developers, university faculty who employ the system, and teacher candidates who have been evaluated based on the TWSM. The key advantages and disadvantages are described below.

### Advantages

The advantages focus on the explicit connection TWSM makes between the act of teaching and the experience of learning by the student:

• *It offers a reasonable method for naturally linking teaching with learning.* "From our viewpoint, there are as many reasons for optimism about TWSM as an approach to measurement as there are reasons for concern . . . .The first of these is the *reasonableness* of the methodology from the perspective of teachers, parents, school administrators, school board members, and the public at large. It anchors to the criterion of ultimate interest (pupil learning), it links pupil learning to teacher work and the realities of the context in which teaching and learning occur, it ensures that measures of pupil learning are connected to what is taught and what pupils are expected to learn, and it provides information about the performance and characteristics of teachers assumed to be related to pupil learning."[25]

  • *The process relies on more naturalistic student learning.* "TWSM is all about teacher learning and student learning, not comparison across groups. It is a homemade measure of teacher work and student work that demonstrates student learning."[26] "Using TWSM, teachers show whether they can develop and employ respectable performance assessments. In high-stakes evaluations, the state and school districts could consider such self-assessment evidence along with a wide range of other more objectively gathered information."[27]

  • *TWSM considers the context of teaching as a major component of teacher assessment.* "The TWSM allows the opportunity to consider the *context* of teaching and learning, for example, analysis of groups, reflection on the setting. It helps explain learning gains (or the lack thereof). Also it helps target the learning needs of all students."[28]

  • *It helps focus the teacher's work on good instruction.* The intent of TWSM is to structure the self-reflective process to enhance instruction. As a result of the analysis, the discussion in a supervisor-teacher meeting can (and should) focus on student learning, which is the essence of good teaching.

  • *It provides alignment between the goals and practice of teaching.* As noted by one teacher we interviewed, "The TWSM helps align the *goals* of teaching with *actual* teaching."[29] "The major advantage of enacting state policies to require the use of work samples is the increased focus on improving and assessing pupil achievement gains."[30]

  • *The teaching-learning connection embeds assessment in daily teaching.* "It informs teacher work and informs students of where they are and where they need to go. It builds capacity to manage one's own learning."[31]

  • *It serves as a valuable tool for formative assessment of teachers.* TWSM is viewed as a way to evaluate what teachers know and are able to do, and as a vehicle to guide professional development.

  • *It encourages teacher reflection and action research.* One of the major benefits of TWSM is that it encourages and even requires the teacher to reflect on the craft of teaching. "My improvement from beginning to end is amazing. [The process] caused me to think about things I would never have thought about."[32]

It provides an opportunity to use "hand-made assessments, provide instruction, then look at the results and reflect on what happened."[33] As Linda Darling-Hammond notes in reviewing the Teacher Work Sample Methodology, "there is value in an approach to teacher assessment that points practitioners to the careful evaluation of practices, contexts, and outcomes, including the systematic consideration of student and teacher work. I have no doubt that this encourages teachers to reflect on their work in ways that are extremely productive for developing diagnostic habits of thinking as well as specific practices."[34]

## Disadvantages

The disadvantages include technical concerns associated with the non-standard nature of performance measures of teacher quality, the time required, and the lack of definition in what is taught and assessed:

• *It is difficult to provide traditional measures of reliability and validity for applied performance measures such as TWSM.* As discussed earlier, traditional measures of reliability and validity are serious concerns in the use of applied performance measures such as Oregon's TWSM. The loosely structured, non-standardized student assessment process inherent in the TWSM makes comparability, consistency, and defensibility serious challenges to overcome.

• *TWSM places a premium on quality teacher-developed measures of student learning, which is a difficult task to achieve in practice.* "One primary concern is the quality of the pre- and post-tests constructed by teachers to assess their pupils' learning."[35] "If assessments are crummy or are not aligned with the curriculum, then the methodology won't demonstrate what was taught."[36]

• *An obvious difficulty is achieving inter-rater reliability with complex samples of teaching.* Although encouraging inter-rater agreement data are summarized earlier in this chapter, this issue will continue to be a challenge in successfully implementing TWSM-type teacher assessment strategies. A partial solution to this dilemma may lie in the better design of methods for scoring teacher work samples and measuring student learning gains. Another potential solution is better training for evaluators. However, reliability concerns are inherent in analyses of qualitative data sources.

• *The ability to assess certain aspects of teaching can dictate what is taught.* The ease and availability of selected assessment strategies has the potential to directly limit both curriculum and instruction in undesirable ways. "*What* can be assessed can determine the goals and objectives: instruction, assessment, student learning cycle. It's important to include more than knowledge acquisition: include concept acquisition and application."[37] It is not clear "to what extent teachers select easy-to-meet objectives or teach narrowly to the specific post-test items. Although it is important to align objectives, instruction, and assessment to one another, it also is important that the objectives themselves be meaningful and worthwhile."[38]

   • *The pre-assessment strategies required in the TWSM can be an unnecessary limiting factor.* "Once goals and objectives, and then pre-assessments, are set, [one] can feel confined to teach that material, even when different learning needs arise. There is a need for flexibility."[39]

   • *Instructional design, development, delivery, and assessment using TWSM require a significant time commitment.* Simply put, "work samples are a lot of work."[40] Not only is this true for the teacher, but also for the administrator who reviews the work samples and provides feedback on the teacher's performance.

   • *Although the TWSM may provide an authentic and in-depth assessment of a given work sample of a teacher, it is too narrow and uncontrolled for making high-stakes decisions.* "It provides too few points to help the student teacher monitor his or her pupils' progress during an instruction unit. As implemented so far, it considers only a small amount of the student-teacher's instruction."[41] "The assessments are not standardized or controlled. Teachers greatly influence what they assess and at what level of performance."[42]

   • *Assessment systems using gain scores have inherent measurement problems.* "The IPG [Index of Pupil Growth] is the index used to measure pupil learning gains. However, it is clear that raw gain scores do not provide a direct indication of the unique contribution a teacher makes to the gains. Other factors such as pupils' prior knowledge, socioeconomic status, student language proficiency, classroom resources, and the like also can influence pupil learning gains."[43]

## What Are the Results of Implementation?

With some cautionary notes, the findings regarding the use of the Oregon Teacher Work Sample Methodology are encouraging. The connection between effective teaching and student learning inherent in the TWSM is logical and a natural outgrowth of teacher work. As one teacher candidate stated, "When I look at what my students are learning, it changes what I am doing and where I am going in my professional development to meet the needs of students."[44]

Results for the use of the work sample methodology to-date include several noteworthy achievements. For one, the evidence collected indicates that TSWM "has strong content and construct validity within the state of Oregon."[45] News like this is encouraging. If the TWSM can be judged to satisfy the rigors of Oregon's standards-based teacher reform effort, then it likely can be adapted for use in standards-based initiatives in other states. In fact, "several states have adopted (and adapted) teacher work sampling as a major piece of either teacher licensure or teacher professional development."[46] Finally, "some of the most promising . . . applications that are emerging for teacher work sample methodology are in the arena of continued teacher development. TWSM is being used both as a professional development tool . . . as well as a tool for evaluating professional development programs . . . ."[47]

Although the Oregon TWSM approach is promising, particularly for beginning teachers, it should be viewed with some caution regarding its application to teacher evaluation. Thus far, the studies conducted have been primarily with teacher candidates, not practicing teachers. Likewise, the focus of the TWSM has been on evaluating the worthiness of aspiring teachers entering the teaching field, not on evaluating the effectiveness of experienced teachers. However, growing evidence indicates that the "accountability" system developed in Oregon for the preparation and licensure of teachers *is* accomplishing the positive results intended:

> It is a system that goes far to ensure the quality and effectiveness of beginning teachers. It focuses teachers . . . on student learning. Finally, it is creating a generation of teachers that have been inducted into a culture of personal and professional responsibility tied to student learning.[48]

## Conclusion

Overall, the Oregon Teacher Work Sample Methodology has received mixed reviews as a useful teacher assessment method. Both significant technical and practical concerns need to be addressed if the process is to receive widespread application. Nonetheless, the potential value of the TWSM model is evident. We believe that the following selection of comments (some from TWSM developers, some from critics of the process) offers a summary reflection on the ability of this approach to link authentic teacher work with student learning:

- "The Western Oregon teacher effectiveness research reflects a growing and appropriate consensus that teacher evaluation should focus squarely on improving pupil achievement."[49]
- "Of equal importance from the perspective of teachers, we believe the methodology and its various applications stand to enhance the professionalization of teaching. Pupil learning is, always has been, and must continue to be the professional touchstone for teachers, and TWSM provides a means for this linkage to be made meaningfully and defensibly."[50]
- "Ironically, TWSM, for all its limitations, is one of the best available teacher evaluation techniques. It is more systematic and useful for assessing teacher effectiveness based on pupil outcome data than are most other practices of teacher evaluation. This is a sobering commentary on the state of teacher evaluation."[51]
- "The Oregon work sampling approach has this to commend it: it actually looks at teaching, and it does so in the context of teachers' goals, classroom contexts, and student learning, measured in ways that attempt to link learning to the educational goals being sought. In these respects, it stands head-and-shoulders above . . . other approaches . . . as a means for providing sound evaluations of teaching that might also be useful in helping teachers improve."[52]

# 4

# Assessing Teacher Quality in a Standards-Based Environment: The Thompson, Colorado, School District

Education is the most powerful weapon which
you can use to change the world.
—Nelson Mandela

The Thompson, Colorado, School District's teacher assessment system is straightforward and considerably less complex and expensive to implement than many models. In fact, we selected it as one of the case studies for the book *because* of its simplicity. The Thompson approach is easy to understand and was implemented within the district's fiscal capacity. Given the quality results that the district has enjoyed with this standards-based teacher assessment system, it should be considered an effective, economically feasible accountability model.

In many respects, the Thompson R2-J School District in Loveland, Colorado, is like so many U.S. school districts: it has unlimited aspirations for its students but limited financial means. Located approximately 40 miles north of Denver and within a few miles of Rocky Mountain National Park, the district is comprised of 28 schools with slightly more than 15,000 students. The 2002–03 annual per pupil expenditure in the district was approximately $5,575, among the lowest within Colorado and low relative to national averages. In addition, teacher salaries were lower than many of the surrounding school districts. Despite the financial limits of the district, historically students have performed relatively higher than comparable SES communities. Nonetheless, parents, school board members, administrators, and teachers in the Loveland educational community believed that students could do better.

## What Are the Purposes of the Assessment System and How Was It Developed?

Consistent with the Colorado State Legislature's requirement that each school district within the state develop a written instrument for evaluating certified school district staff members,[1] and early in the evaluation development process,[2] the Thompson Board of Education adopted the following belief statement to guide the expectations, design, and implementation of the teacher evaluation system:

> The Board of Education, administration, staff, and parents are committed to providing and maintaining the best possible education for our students. An important indicator of an excellent educational program is the competence and professionalism of the district's instructional staff. The district recognizes that the instructional process is extremely complex, and the appraisal of the school professional's performance is a challenging endeavor *but critical to the educational goals, achievement*, and well-being of our students. [*emphasis added*]

In addition to this over-arching belief statement, the board adopted several specific beliefs regarding the evaluation system, the first of which reads: "The School Professional Evaluation and Supervision Process should focus on the enhancement of student achievement and well-being." Thus, the Thompson School District Professional Evaluation System is squarely focused on the district's overarching goals of continued improvement in student achievement.

### Designing the Evaluation System

Given this background of relatively low fiscal capacity and a commitment to quality academic performance, in 1993 the local school board began investigating ways to attract and retain well-qualified teachers *and* increase student achievement. With strong community support and encouragement, the school board initially considered a pay-for-performance program to resolve these dual challenges.

Work began in the 1993–94 school year with the creation of a "Performance Pay Design Committee." Members were selected jointly by the school district administration and the local NEA affiliate. Shortly after its formation, the committee solicited input from the business community regarding performance pay. Next, focus group meetings were conducted with major stakeholders in an effort to understand what the greater community desired from its schools. Additionally, the committee surveyed teachers and parents in every school to gather their perceptions on how to improve the schools. Based on the findings from this year-long data gathering effort, and with strong community support, the committee shifted away from merely considering pay-for-performance to a more systemic school improvement process.

Beginning with the 1994–95 school year, the committee continued its work with a broadened school improvement mission and a specific focus on designing an effective performance assessment system. The committee invested considerable effort in designing teacher job performance standards and developing implementation procedures for the evaluation system. Then, the committee submitted a draft evaluation system to independent reviewers. Following revisions suggested from the draft review, the committee presented the teacher standards and evaluation system to teachers and administrators for their consideration.

## Piloting and Staff Development

A two-year pilot process began the following academic year, with major revisions made following the evaluation of the system after the first year, and minor modifications made after the second. Following this extensive four-year planning, development, and piloting sequence, the school board was ready to implement the new standards-based teacher evaluation system district-wide.

As the school district moved toward full implementation at the inception of the 1997–98 school year, one final step was taken: administrator and teacher training. All school administrators participated in a three-day training program designed to introduce the new system and build technical skills in areas related to school improvement and teacher evaluation. The skill building components for supervisors included

- An introduction to more effective approaches to supervision and teacher coaching,
- Role-playing to provide hands-on experience with the new evaluation system,
- Instruction on how to conduct effective pre- and postobservation conferences,
- Guidance on supporting data-driven instruction, and
- Discussion of strategies for monitoring performance in a standards-based teacher assessment system.

Following administrator training, a train-the-trainers model was used with teacher leaders representing all schools to introduce the system to the district's teachers. In addition to teacher leaders receiving technical training with the new evaluation system, the program devoted energy to "eliminating worst fears and debugging rumors" during teacher training.[3] Finally, the teacher leaders and principals delivered training to all teachers in each respective building. The new teacher evaluation system was officially launched.

## How Does the Assessment System Work?

Under the umbrella of increasing student achievement and well-being,[4] the key components in the teacher evaluation system are designed to logically connect teacher and student expectations, and are fairly straightforward:

- Teacher performance standards
- A district teacher evaluation system
- Teacher professional development and performance improvement

### Teacher Performance Standards

The evaluation system begins with the identification of 10 teacher professional standards,[5] for which all teachers are held accountable and against which their performance is measured. Among others, these include expectations such as "demonstrates the basic components of effective instruction . . . ," "designs and implements instruction to meet the unique needs of students . . . ," and "communicates with students, families . . . concerning student academic and behavioral progress."[6] Figure 4.1 provides a complete list of these teacher professional standards.

While these standards infer a connection between teacher performance and student learning, it is Standard 3 that makes this expectation explicit: "The school professional is responsible for increasing the probability of advancing student achievement."[7] The expectation is clear: teachers and other education professionals will be held accountable for student learning.

## Evaluation Implementation Procedures

The evaluation system has a direct link to student achievement, but only as *one factor* in the teacher's performance review. In addition to direct measures of student learning, other sources include formal and informal observations, self-evaluation, and reviews of artifacts related to job performance. This multiple-source data collection process culminates in an annual summative evaluation conference during which judgments are made regarding the teacher's performance in the evaluation cycle.

## Professional Development

In addition to assessing performance against the 10 teacher professional standards, the summative evaluation conference provides an opportunity to connect the performance of teachers with their professional development needs in the upcoming evaluation cycle. Figure 4.2 summarizes key protocols that are available for use by teachers and principals during the evaluation process, several of which relate either directly or indirectly to teacher professional improvement. Each of the accompanying forms for the processes in Figure 4.2 is provided in Appendix D.

Ultimately, from professional standards to performance assessment to professional growth and improvement, the entire standards-based evaluation system is predicated on improving student achievement. Teacher professional growth is viewed as the key to success in this improvement cycle. An underlying assumption of the Thompson assessment system is that if teacher performance continually improves and is of high quality, then student academic performance will improve.

---

**FIGURE 4.1**
**Thompson School District Teacher Professional Standards**

---

*These are the behaviors that a school professional must exhibit consistently over time to maintain employment in the Thompson R2-J School District. These standards are evaluated on an annual basis.*

1. **The school professional consistently demonstrates the basic components of effective instruction and uses other instructional models as appropriate.**
   a. Develops plans to support instructional or training objectives.
   b. Demonstrates instruction or training that includes initial focus, appropriate delivery, guided and independent practice, monitoring of instruction, and a closing, or uses other instructional models as appropriate.
   c. Provides a variety of formative and summative assessments that measure student progress toward objectives.
   d. Designs and implements management processes that are conducive to student learning.

2. **The school professional provides a program of instruction or training in accordance with the adopted curriculum and consistent with state standards and federal and state regulations.**
   a. Uses district curriculum guidelines in planning and implementing instruction.
   b. Demonstrates a connection between teacher-prepared lessons or units and district curriculum standards.
   c. Is knowledgeable about scope and sequence of district curriculum standards as applicable.

3. **The school professional is responsible for increasing the probability of advancing student achievement.**
   a. Collects and analyzes student data to drive instruction.
   b. Uses multiple measures to document student growth.
   c. Implements strategies based on various types of student achievement data to improve student performance.
   d. Analyzes the results of instruction and modifies instruction accordingly.
   e. Organizes a learning environment to maximize the potential for student time on task.

4. **The school professional designs and implements instruction to meet the unique needs of students.**
   a. Makes decisions about and provides instructional materials and strategies that address a variety of learning needs.
   b. Describes students' current performance levels and future instructional needs.
   c. Designs and provides a variety of performance opportunities that demonstrate student learning.
   d. Uses prescribed modifications for special populations.

5. **The school professional recognizes, develops, and maintains an environment conducive to student well being.**
   a. Encourages and models respect for all students.
   b. Creates a learning environment in which students can feel safe taking the risks necessary for learning.

*(continued)*

**FIGURE 4.1**
**(continued)**

   c. Encourages student interactions that promote personal growth and self-worth.
   d. Respects the cultural and learning diversity of students.

6. **The school professional communicates with students, families, colleagues, and community members concerning student academic and behavioral progress.**
   a. Listens with intent to understand.
   b. Clearly defines and communicates expectations to students and families.
   c. Works to establish partnerships and maintain communication with students, families, colleagues, and community members with respect to student strengths, needs, and progress.
   d. Communicates individual student needs in a confidential manner where appropriate.
   e. Is articulate, selecting works with clarity and precision.

7. **The school professional assists in upholding and enforcing school rules, Board of Education policies, federal and state rules and regulations, and adheres to licensure standards.**
   a. Can access copies of and comply with school rules, Board of Education policies, federal and state rules and regulations, and licensure standards.
   b. Monitors student behavior in accordance with building, district, federal, and state policies, and takes appropriate action.

8. **The school professional maintains records as required by law, district policy, and administrative regulations in a timely and confidential manner.**
   a. Completes required forms, reports, and plans according to district policies.
   b. Documents student behavior and academic progress for appropriate placement or referral.
   c. Submits forms, reports, and plans in a timely manner.

9. **The school professional demonstrates professional cooperative relationships with others.**
   a. Asks for assistance or provides colleagues and families with assistance and collaborates on meeting individual student needs.
   b. Uses conflict resolution and decision-making processes to solve problems in the work place.
   c. Shares information, materials, and expertise with colleagues.

10. **The school professional exhibits professional employment characteristics.**
   a. Meets and instructs students in the location at the time designated according to job assignment, with as few absences as possible.
   b. Performs related duties as assigned by the administration in accordance with district policies and practices.
   c. Attends and participates in required meetings.
   d. Models appropriate behavior in the school setting according to district policy.

**FIGURE 4.2**
**List of Thompson Teacher Evaluation Tools**

| Protocol | Description |
|---|---|
| Teacher Professional Standards | The 10 professional standards describe the behaviors that a school professional must exhibit consistently over time to maintain employment in the Thompson School District. The standards are evaluated on an annual basis. |
| Pre-observation: Standards-Based Planning | This form is used for teachers to <br>• List the subject area of the observation, <br>• Identify the standard or benchmark that will be addressed, and <br>• Describe the concept of the lesson. |
| Pre-observation: Data-Driven Instruction Planning | This is a self-evaluation tool for new teachers or teachers in a new role. It can be used to help a teacher prepare for an observation and conference. |
| Pre-observation: Standards-Based Classrooms | This is a tool for note taking during the conference or to have the teacher fill out prior to observation. Administrators can use the tool to note evidence of data-driven instruction. |
| Self-Evaluation: Using New Instructional Strategies | This tool may be useful to new teachers or teachers in a new role as a postobservation tool. It also may be useful as an indicator for teachers to document professional goals. Administrators may use this tool for reflection in postobservation or goal development conferences. |
| Pre- and Post-Observation: Using a Variety of Instructional Strategies | This can be used as a self-evaluation tool for school professionals, and as a pre- or postobservation tool. Administrators may use these prompts for reflection in postobservation or goal development conferences. |
| Pre-Observation: Planning for Assessment | This instrument is used by the teacher to measure student learning as it relates to the benchmark for a given lesson. |
| Data Collection: Using Expectations and Assessments in Instruction | This instrument can be used to evaluate the quality of a teacher's classroom assessment process. The evaluator can use specific examples of tests, analysis of assessment, or observe the results of the assessment of data in the form of lesson plans based on those data. |
| Reflection on the Assessment Plan | This is a postobservation form to be filled out by the teacher or to guide a postobservation conference. |
| Professional Growth Plans | This self-evaluation tool can be used by a teacher for monitoring the progress of his professional goals. Administrators may use the form for reflection questions, general data collection, or goal development conferences. Evidence, observations, or examples can be cited and indicators checked. The school professional uses a written professional development plan as a guide to self-improvement and learning and then analyzes the results of that plan. |

## What Are the Student Assessment Strategies?

A gain-score approach to student assessment is employed that can be expressed as:

Student's ending achievement level —
Beginning achievement level = Gain score

The district personnel consider student assessment from the perspective of measuring student growth, not taking snapshots of test performance with different cohorts of students.* Thus, their approach is a value-added perspective.

In this type of gain-score environment, the following sequence of events unfolds:

- Step 1: The student's baseline performance is determined.
- Step 2: The teacher provides "data-driven" instruction.
- Step 3: The student's postinstruction performance is assessed.
- Step 4: The growth in achievement is documented.

The framework for the "data-driven" instruction process[8] is cyclical and includes the following steps:

1. Start with *content standards*.
2. Create and find *assessment* aligned to content standards.
3. Assess for *diagnostic* purposes.
4. Analyze the *data*.
5. Identify the *learning styles* of students.
6. Plan for a variety of *teaching and learning strategies* and environments.
7. Implement the *instruction;* monitor and adjust as needed.
8. *Administer* assessment for evaluation.

---

*Too often school districts administer a single point-in-time test near the end of the course or year. Then, they use these test results to measure "progress" for the district, schools, and even individual classrooms. This approach, unfortunately, results in making comparisons among different groups of students rather than their work at different stages. Thompson avoids this problem by considering where students are at the beginning of the year, where they are at the end, and what is the difference.

Assessment in the data-driven instruction process takes place with guid-ance from the district regarding which tests to use and when to use them. However, the classroom teacher has considerable latitude in deciding how and when to use classroom assessments as part of student assessment performance.

Beginning in kindergarten and extending through 12th grade, a wide array of both standardized and informal measures are used to assess student performance. Operationally, the student performance assessments can be grouped into four categories[9]:

1. State standards assessment: annual tests given to grades 3–10 that are aligned with Colorado's content standards.

2. Norm-referenced tests (e.g., PSAT and SAT).

3. Criterion-referenced tests (e.g., reading or math levels, science process skills, and proficiency).

4. Classroom assessments: teacher-made classroom assessments including multiple choice, essay, performance tasks, and demonstrations.

See Chapter 2 for an explanation of how to use the various types of tests in student assessment.

## What Are the Advantages and Disadvantages of the Assessment System?

In an effort to assess the advantages and disadvantages of a standards-based teacher evaluation program, we interviewed a cross-section of Thompson's educational community. Additionally, we reviewed the school district's eval-uation documents and considered design elements and results of the pro-gram. The following is a summary of these findings.

### Advantages

The advantages reflect a tighter connection among instruction, student learning, and teacher professional growth. The focus on student learning appears to anchor the professional work of educators:

- *There is a clear focus on student learning needs.* "We focus more on what students need to learn, not covering the curriculum."[10] "If you look at data-driven student learning, you get better results than going with what the publisher says the next chapter should be. . . .Teachers are employing research-based instruction."[11]

- *The standards-based approach to evaluation supports a feeling of professionalism.* "Evaluation systems historically have talked process, not outcomes. The primary advantage is that you get people to reexamine their beliefs about what is good for children."[12] "[There is an] assumption that professionals have a certain level of knowledge and that changes can be made in response to student achievement."[13]

- *The evaluation system provides a customer focus.* "Students are the customers; parents and community are key stakeholders."[14]

- *The evaluation system helps motivate teachers.* "[The evaluation system] makes teachers feel better . . . when you see the results, you know you've helped kids."[15]

- *Teacher collegiality is encouraged.* "It has given a lot more collegiality in professional development."[16] "You can't do this without sharing [thus, some of the isolation of teaching is removed]."[17] "[The evaluation system] increases quality interactions among professionals: principal-to-teacher and teacher-to-teacher."[18]

- *The standards for evaluation are clearer.* "It is clear what teachers are being evaluated on and takes away a lot of the subjectivity."[19]

- *Teacher performance improvement is emphasized.* "[In] data-driven or data-influenced decision making, we can find what some of our best practices are to improve student achievement and replicate them."[20] "If we aren't encouraging low-performing employees to improve, we're accepting a level of mediocrity."[21]

- *Staff development is more directly connected to student learning needs.* "If you look at data-driven staff development, you increase the probability of improving student learning."[22]

## Disadvantages

The disadvantages involve concerns about the technical aspects of assessment (reliability and validity) plus the time and skills necessary to make assessment an integral part of instruction without compromising content or creativity:

- *This evaluation approach allows for significant variability in implementation.* "The system is only as good as the practitioner."[23]
- *The evaluation system can stifle risk taking and creativity.* "My major concern is that teachers will interpret the importance of test performance in a 'drill-and-kill' instructional approach that is overly narrow. We need a moderate approach."[24]
- *The multitiered student assessment system lacks stringent statistical controls.* "[There is] confusion about the multiple assessments that can be used to measure student learning."[25] "We have a primitive data base from which to work with value-added impact of teaching. Knowledge of educational effectiveness is limited in being able to account for all learning factors."[26]
- *Clear-cut and comparable measures of student improvement are difficult to obtain.* "[It is] difficult to determine the vehicle to measure student growth that is acceptable by teachers, administrators, and the community."[27]
- *The system requires a significant time commitment to student assessment.* "When doing a lot of student assessment, what gives is teaching time. Teacher scheduling and planning is complicated by so much testing."[28] ". . . more time in testing, more research to get the scores, more time in developing ways to assess."[29]
- *Teachers can perceive an evaluation system based on student achievement as threatening.* "It's scary to a lot of teachers to be evaluated on how our students achieve."[30] "[There are] very long-standing concerns of elements outside of school that influence student learning."[31]
- *Public reporting of test results creates stress.* "There is pressure from public reporting [of] test results . . . ."[32] "[There is] stress in getting your score and reading them in the paper the same night."[33]
- *The financial demands are substantial.* "There is a huge budgetary impact to focus on improving student test scores."[34] (For example, because the Thompson system relies on teacher-based assessment of student progress and not just standardized norm- or criterion-referenced tests, the professional development investment in teacher assessment skills is expensive and unending.)

## What Are the Results of Implementation?

One clear and significant disadvantage inherent in a standards-based teacher evaluation system is the difficulty in directly and precisely attributing student performance to teacher performance. Nonetheless, when the Thompson model is viewed in its totality, the evaluation system appears successful. Although district administrators can only approximate the impact of a given teacher's influence on student learning, they definitely can point to the overall outcome of the experience: student learning as measured by standardized test scores is increasing.

As evidence of the demonstrated increase in student performance, school officials point to the progress of Thompson students on the Colorado State Assessment Program (CSAP). In 1997, 65 percent of Thompson's 4th grade students scored at or above proficiency level (proficient or advanced) on the CSAP reading test. In 2001, 75 percent scored at or above proficiency, a performance increase that yielded the highest learning growth rank among Colorado's 176 school districts. Similarly, in 1997, 35 percent of Thompson's 4th graders passed the CSAP writing assessment at or above the proficient level, and in 2001, 57 percent scored proficient or higher. Thompson's 7th graders achieved comparably impressive achievement results across the period 1999–2001. The percent of 7th graders scoring proficient or advanced in reading in 1999 was 69 percent; in 2001, the rate was 75 percent. Also, in 1999, 58 percent of 7th graders passed the writing assessment at proficiency or advanced; in 2001, 65 percent were at proficiency or advanced.

In addition to the hard evidence of rising student achievement scores, an apparent peripheral benefit is a heightened awareness district-wide in the importance of focusing on student results. One of the central office administrators summed up this attitude by stating:

> Student achievement has been on the rise; we continue to show growth. Students in their own language are talking about standards. They know what is expected of them and what they should be able to do.[35]

Responding from a classroom perspective, one elementary teacher summarized the impact of the teacher-student assessment system on her students thusly:

> I'm more aware of how my students are achieving. I have data, now, to show parents how their children are learning. It is based more on hard data and not on feelings. It's not just instinct—it's *provable*.[36]

**Teacher Perspectives**

Although teachers expressed caveats in their comments, those who had participated in Thompson's standards-based teacher assessment system were quite positive. The following comments are indicative of teacher responses to this question:

• "I would go with it absolutely, *if* [it were] based on student growth. That is what our job is, to teach children, and teaching means students should learn. [However], can you measure every part of student learning? No. Teachers need to make every effort for student growth to occur, but other factors have to be accounted for."[37]

• "As long as it's understood that you don't have total control [of the student's learning]."[38]

• "Yes. I absolutely believe we should be held accountable. If students aren't learning, we should be able to document what we have done to encourage their learning."[39]

# Conclusion

As with any teacher evaluation system, distinct advantages and disadvantages are embedded in Thompson's standards-based approach. The system is now several years old. Thompson school officials are considering revisions beginning in 2004–05 to further refine and improve it; however, many technical-rational components of the evaluation model as it exists now are worth considering. In addition, the teachers interviewed and the superintendent of schools offered nearly identical observations regarding the process of change that bear repeating: *To bring about this change, there must be a collaborative partnership between teachers and administrators. There must be trust.* The Thompson School District model requires a high level of professional accountability for its educators and is heavily reliant on a supportive and trusting environment that truly focuses on improvement for everyone in the system. Striking the right balance of accountability and support within schools is probably the greatest challenge that school leaders face.

# 5

# Assessing Teacher Quality Through Goal-Setting: The Alexandria, Virginia, School District

Melissa McBride and Mason Miller

Goals determine what you are going to be.
—Julius Irving

In 2000, the Alexandria City Public School system implemented the Performance Evaluation Program (PEP), a comprehensive teacher evaluation system with four components: formal observations, informal observations, teacher portfolios, and academic goal-setting. The decision to design a new evaluation system drawn from multiple data sources was driven by the call for accountability within the Commonwealth of Virginia and by the desire to paint an "authentic portrait" of the complex nature of teaching. PEP seeks to link teacher evaluation to student achievement via the academic goal-setting component, which requires teachers to set annual quantifiable goals related to their students' progress. Throughout the school year, goals are reviewed by PEP specialists and administrators. Similar to the Thompson School District evaluation model, the Alexandria City Public School district endeavors to answer the call for accountability via the connection of teacher evaluation and professional development with the goal of increased student learning, which is described in the next chapter. Since its inception in 2000, only 9 of the 18 schools have fully implemented all components of the program. Although full, district-wide implementation of the PEP will not occur until the start of the 2004–05 school year, all schools have been involved in the academic goal-setting component of PEP since the autumn of 2003.

## A Brief Description of the Alexandria City School District

Alexandria, Virginia, is a seaport city located within the greater metropolitan area of Washington, D.C. Regarded as a smaller school district within the Commonwealth of Virginia, the school system is comprised of 18 K–12 schools and serves approximately 11,000 students from diverse ethnic and socioeconomic backgrounds. Student demographics as of September 30, 2003 were as follows:

- Black                                    43.00 percent
- Hispanic                                 27.00 percent
- White                                    23.02 percent
- Asian/Pacific Islander                    6.70 percent
- American Indian/Alaskan Native            0.30 percent

Eighty-eight countries of origin are represented and 69 different languages are spoken in Alexandria's classrooms.[1] Roughly 25 percent of the total student population (approximately 2,625 students) has been identified as Limited English Proficient (ESL students).[2] Fifty-one percent (5,493 students) of Alexandria public school students are eligible for free and reduced-price lunch meals.[3] Over 50 percent of the student body is considered "at-risk" and require additional services. In addition, approximately 15 percent (1,641 students) are eligible for special services.[4] In light of these major challenges to student learning, the Alexandria City Public School system dedicates 85 percent of its budget (approx. $123,094,863) to instruction and instructional support.[5]

Alexandria is a technology-rich school district with a student-to-computer ratio of 3:1,[6] far exceeding the Commonwealth of Virginia's student-to-computer ratio of 6:1. The average teacher salary is greater than the state mean, $54,224 versus $41,731 respectively.[7] Average classroom size ranges between 20 and 23 students.[8] Above all, Alexandria City Public School educators are passionate about their students' success.

## What Are the Purposes of the Assessment System and How Was It Developed?

Influenced by the intensifying "call for tangible evidence of student learning"[9] within the Commonwealth of Virginia and nationally, the Alexandria school board initially was interested in developing a merit pay system that integrated some measure of student achievement. However, the use of student achievement data in teacher appraisal systems remains controversial.[10] Many within the district feared that implementing a merit pay system would polarize the educational community. "We did not want this to be an evaluation system that was an 'I gotcha!' We wanted it to be a system that *really* promoted professional growth."[11] Although teachers and administrators were somewhat uncomfortable with the idea of using measures of student learning in the evaluation process, they perceived this as a challenge they needed to embrace.

Designing the new evaluation program was a collaborative effort among several internal stakeholders within the Alexandria school district: teachers and principals ranging from the elementary to the secondary levels of education, and central office administrators who worked with James H. Stronge as a consultant for the development process. The new performance assessment process is based on the Goals and Roles Evaluation Model,[12] a six-step approach to performance assessment. The development team reviewed, and in some instances adapted, evaluation materials from 11 public school divisions within the Commonwealth of Virginia and one school in Michigan. A complete listing of these school divisions is provided in Appendix E.

Adhering to the advice of researchers in the field that student data be used "as only one component of a teacher evaluation system that is based on multiple data sources,"[13] the architects of the Alexandria system strove to build one that was comprehensive and recognized the complexities of teaching. Five main data sources were chosen: formal observations, informal observations, portfolios, goal-setting, and student achievement. Definitions of each data source are presented in Figure 5.1. The designers felt that an

**FIGURE 5.1**
**Definitions of Main Data Sources**

| Data Source | Definition |
|---|---|
| Goal-Setting | Teachers have a definite impact on student learning and academic performance. Depending on grade level, content area, and ability level, appropriate measures of student performance are identified to provide information on the learning gains of students. Performance measures include standardized test results as well as other pertinent data. |
| Student Achievement | Teachers set goals for improving student achievement based on appropriate performance measures. The goals and the goal fulfillment are important data sources for evaluation. |
| Formal Observations | Observations are an important source of performance information. Formal observations focus directly on 17 teacher performance responsibilities (see page 59). Classroom observations may also include review of teacher products or artifacts. |
| Informal Observations | Informal observations are intended to provide more frequent information on a wider variety of contributions made by the teacher. Evaluators are encouraged to conduct informal observations by visiting classrooms, observing instruction, and observing work in non-classroom settings at various times. |
| Portfolios | The portfolio includes artifacts that provide documentation for the 17 performance responsibilities. |

*Source:* Reprinted with permission from Alexandria City Public Schools.

"authentic portrait of the teacher's work"[14] would be painted by these multiple data sources. It is the first two data sources, goal-setting and student achievement, on which this chapter is focused. The purpose of academic goal-setting *is* to

• Establish a positive correlation between the quality of teaching and learning,
• Make instructional decisions based upon student data,
• Create a mechanism for school improvement, and
• Increase effectiveness of instruction via continuous professional growth.

Conversely, the purpose of academic goal-setting *is not* to

• Replace classroom observations or other means of documenting performance or
• Be utilized as the sole measure of teacher effectiveness.

Additionally, it is important to understand that Alexandria's academic goal-setting process is not the creation of a teacher's personal or professional goals (e.g., "I plan to improve instruction through . . . ," or "I plan to complete a master's degree."). Rather, the academic goal-setting process is explicitly focused on student academic progress:

1. Where are students in terms of academic progress at the beginning of the school year?
2. What am I planning to do to help this group of students succeed this year?
3. Where are the students at mid-year?
4. Where are students, in terms of academic progress, at the end of the school year?
5. How much progress did the students make?

Thus, in a very direct sense, the Alexandria City Public School Performance Evaluation Program incorporates a value-added approach to student learning that can be applied to teachers at various grade levels and in different subjects.

## How Does the Assessment System Work?

As noted earlier, academic goal-setting is one of five components in the PEP. The other components are (1) student achievement, (2) formal observations, (3) informal observations, and (4) teacher portfolios. In recent years, substantial research has indicated that teacher effectiveness is the strongest school-based predictor of student achievement.[15] To better understand the goal-setting component of PEP and how it relates to evaluating teacher effectiveness, it is imperative to outline the guiding principles of the Alexandria teacher evaluation system.

Adapting Stronge's Goals and Roles Evaluation Model,[16] the Alexandria PEP examines teacher performance via a three-tiered approach (Figure 5.2). Five general domains, or categories, provide a conceptual framework: instruction, assessment, learning environment, communications and community relations, and professionalism. A table defining each of the teacher performance domains is provided in Appendix E. The following example is the definition of the Assessment domain:

> This domain includes the processes of gathering, reporting, and using a variety of data in a consistent manner to measure achievement, plan instruction, and improve student performance.[17]

A total of 17 performance responsibilities exist for teachers; a listing of these within their respective domains is provided in Appendix E. The following is an example of a performance responsibility within the Assessment domain:

> Performance Responsibility A-3: The teacher provides ongoing and timely feedback to encourage student progress.[18]

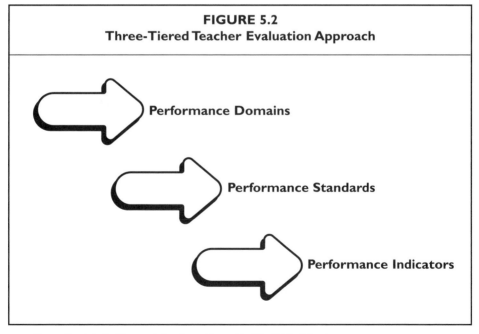

**FIGURE 5.2**
**Three-Tiered Teacher Evaluation Approach**

Performance Domains

Performance Standards

Performance Indicators

*Source:* Reprinted with permission from Alexandria City Public Schools.

Performance indicators have been developed for each performance responsibility and are used to identify observable behaviors of the major job expectations. The lists of sample behaviors are not exhaustive, but they illustrate the typical actions that indicate satisfactory implementation of a performance responsibility. Examples of performance indicators for Performance Responsibility A-3 follow, in which the teacher

- Gives performance feedback to students before, during, and after instruction,
- Collects sufficient assessment data to support accurate reports of student progress, and
- Provides opportunities for students to assess their own progress and performance.

Data are collected through observation, portfolio review, goal-setting, and student performance measures to provide the most comprehensive and accurate feedback on teacher performance. Evaluators use two tools to complete teachers' summative evaluations: the performance indicators and the performance rubric. The performance rubric is based upon a behavioral summary scale. It guides evaluators in an effort to increase inter-rater reliability (the consistency of ratings by different supervisors). The rubric is a four-level continuum that ranges from "exceeds expectations" to "unsatisfactory."

## What Are the Student Assessment Strategies?

Student performance measures are vital to the goal-setting process. Teachers can use gathered student information as evidence of fulfilling a specific responsibility. Teachers have a variety of measures for gauging student progress. To accommodate the wide variety of learners, all three of the following criteria are considered when selecting appropriate measures of learning: grade level, content area, and ability level of students. The focus is to select student assessment measures that are closely aligned with the curriculum. The following is a list of assessment strategies and examples of data sources to be used for the documentation of student learning:

- Norm-referenced tests (e.g., Stanford Diagnostic Reading Test [SDRT4])
- Criterion-referenced tests (e.g., Phonemic Awareness Literacy Screening [PALS])

- Authentic assessments (e.g., portfolios, projects, writing assessments)
- In-house tests (e.g., district-wide quarterly tests, teacher-made tests)
- Standards-based assessments (e.g., Virginia Standards of Learning [SOL])

## How Is the Assessment System Related to Teacher Evaluation?

Virginia state law requires that the performance evaluation of instructional personnel include measures of student academic progress:

> School boards shall develop a procedure for use by division superintendents and principals in evaluating instructional personnel that is appropriate to the tasks performed and addresses, among other things, student academic progress and the skills and knowledge of instructional personnel, including, but not limited to, instructional methodology, classroom management, and subject matter knowledge. (§22.1-295)[19]

Although academic goal-setting is not mandatory, it is one reasonable method of satisfying the Commonwealth's requirement. In the goal-setting process, teachers must link their goals to one or more of the 17 teacher responsibilities. At the beginning of each school year, tenured and non-tenured teachers collaborate with administrators and PEP specialists to develop at least one goal for improving student learning. In order to define annual goals that are SMART (specific, measurable, attainable, realistic, and timebound), teachers first do the following:

- Collect and review student and teacher evaluation data.
- Analyze the data selected to determine student and professional needs.
- Interpret the data looking for patterns or areas of weakness.
- Determine the areas of need based upon these concrete data sources.
- Select a focus for the goals.

Data that are collected and reviewed include student test results, previous teacher evaluations, and teacher portfolios. Teachers and PEP specialists work together to identify areas of student performance and instruction that require improvement. Once patterns are identified, teachers select areas that they would like to improve for both themselves and their students. Again, this determination is based upon concrete data sources. The overarching purpose of these steps is to identify and define a baseline of performance for teachers and their students. The actual development of goals involves the following steps:

1. *Define a clear objective.*
   - Use a specific assessment strategy or type of performance.
   - Set a measurable target (e.g., percent, number correct).
2. *Select assessment strategies that are aligned with the goal.*
   - Collect data before and after instruction (if possible).
   - Use multiple measures of student learning to analyze and verify results.
3. *End-of-the-Year Review*
   - Make adjustments where appropriate (e.g., instruction, groupings).

Annual goals are customized for each teacher and include specific information in order to accommodate the context in which teaching and learning occur, thereby enabling the evaluator to make a more appropriate assessment of the teacher's performance. Goals include the following information:

- Demographic information about the teacher (e.g., content area, grade level, school).
- Baseline information about the students (e.g., pre-test scores, attendance records, standardized test scores, gifted, at-risk).
- Goal statement describing desired results.
- Strategies that have been selected to accomplish the goal.
- Progress report at mid-year or at other appropriate intervals.
- Summary of end-of-year accomplishments.[20]

The following examples are provided to assist the reader in visualizing the design of an annual goal. Figure 5.3 is one form teachers may use to document a goal. Teachers complete these forms in collaboration with the PEP specialist. Figure 5.4 is an example of an actual annual goal.

Teachers are encouraged to organize and display their students' academic progress by using the following sources:

- Tables of raw student data by class and their assessment scores.
- Tables of compiled data (e.g., percent of students at a certain benchmark, such as proficiency level).

---

**FIGURE 5.3**
**Sample Goal-Setting Form**

---

*Alexandria City Public Schools*
Teacher Annual Goals for Improving Student Achievement

Teacher _____ Evaluator_____

Grade/Subject _____ School Year _____

School_____

**Setting** *[Describe the population and special learning circumstances.]*

**Content Area** *[The area/topic I will address (e.g., reading instruction, long division, problem solving).]*

**Baseline Data** *[Where I am now (e.g., status at beginning of year).]*

**Goal Statement** *[What I want to accomplish this year (i.e., my desired results).]*

**Strategies for Improvement** *[Activities I will use to accomplish my goal.]*

_____

Evaluator's Signature/Date                    Teacher's Signature/Date

- - - - - - - - - - - - - - - - - - - - - - - - - - - - - - - - - - - - - - - - - - - - - - - - - - - - - - - - - - - - - - - - - -

**End-of-Year Data and Results** *[Accomplishments by year-end.]*

*Source:* Reprinted with permission from Alexandria City Public Schools.

---

**FIGURE 5.4**
**Example of Completed Goal-Setting Form**

Teacher Annual Goals for Improving Student Achievement

Teacher <u>Blaise Pascal</u>        Evaluator <u>Mrs. Humane</u>

Grade/Subject <u>9 Algebra I</u>        School Year <u>2002–2003</u>

School <u>James Madison H.S.</u>

**Setting** *[Describe the population and special learning circumstances.]*
James Madison High School is located in an urban setting and has an enrollment of 1,920 students in grades 9–12 with an average daily attendance of 91 percent and a Free/Reduced Lunch rate of 40 percent. In 2001–02, 37 percent of the students passed the end-of-course SOL Algebra I test (compared to 27 percent in 2000–01).

**Content Area** *[The area/topic I will address (e.g., reading instruction, long division, problem solving).]*
Instruction — Algebra I

**Baseline Data** *[Where I am now (e.g., status at beginning of year).]*
Test results in 2002–03 indicate that the total math average gain for my five classes is 10.54 compared to the division norm of 15.6, the problem-solving gain is 9.6 compared to the division norm of 17.4, and the procedures gain is 11.96 compared to 13.8. Overall, my classes are near the division norm for procedures but are low in problem solving, which reduces the total math results.

**Goal Statement** *[What I want to accomplish this year (i.e., my desired results).]*
I will meet or exceed division norms for the total average math gain in my five classes using the Tests for Accountability. I will show an improvement of 4 points average gain or more in the problem-solving subscale scores on the same test.

**Strategies for Improvement** *[Activities I will use to accomplish my goal.]*
I will work with the mentor teacher and math department chair to infuse more problem-solving activities in my lesson plans, along with supportive instructional strategies such as cooperative work groups, use of manipulatives, and student explanations of the problems. I will ask the mentor teacher to work closely with me and offer demonstration lessons, team-teaching opportunities, and opportunities to visit other Algebra I classrooms.

_____

Evaluator's Signature/Date        Teacher's Signature/Date

- - - - - - - - - - - - - - - - - - - - - - - - - - - - - - - - - - - - - - - - - - - - - - - - - - - - - -

**End-of-Year Data and Results** *[Accomplishments by year-end.]*

*Source:* Reprinted with permission from Alexandria City Public Schools.

• Graphs of compiled data (e.g., pie charts, stacked graphs).
• Simultaneous graphing of multiple measures (e.g., a mix of various standardized measures).

### Staff Development

The design of the Performance Evaluation Program emphasizes both formative and summative aspects of evaluation. In particular, the goal-setting component relies on continuous feedback and staff development that complements the teachers' annual goals. PEP specialists play an important role in this program, working with teachers to design goals based upon student data and assisting in the selection of appropriate instructional strategies to achieve these goals. PEP specialists also provide continuous support and lead staff training on various aspects of the goal-setting process throughout the year, which is necessary to ensure that student data are appropriately used and interpreted.

### Safeguards

The goal-setting process is just one component of the PEP; no adverse personnel decisions are based solely on the failure of teachers to achieve their annual goals. Teacher evaluation is no longer something that is "done to them," such as a 10-minute observation. Instead, the architects designed it to be a collaborative effort among teachers, evaluators, and PEP specialists. Regarding the goal-setting process specifically, teachers are empowered to determine the selection of their own goals and student assessment measures. The intention is to provide professional development and support to improve the effectiveness of instruction. "There has been personnel *interaction* [based on goal-setting], but not action."[21]

## What Are the Advantages and Disadvantages of the Assessment System?

In determining the advantages and disadvantages of the student achievement academic goal-setting component of Alexandria's PEP program, interviews were conducted with central office administrators, instructional specialists, principals, and teachers, and the relevant information was incorporated.

## Advantages

The advantages cited focused primarily on the reflective and collaborative aspects of the goal-setting process:

• *Encourages teacher reflection and data-driven decision making.* "It makes you reflect on your practice and how to come up with better ways to do things."[22] "Importance is placed on how the strategies come to life in the classroom context."[23] "Instead of just looking at scores, we look (now) at test questions. So, now my goals are related to more specific content areas that I want to improve."[24]

• *Fosters teacher collaboration and collegiality.* "We are discussing it a lot more amongst ourselves. Our PEP specialist had us go around and talk about our individual goals. It was really helpful to hear what somebody else was doing, and we could offer up suggestions."[25] "I think the biggest thing that has changed my style of teaching is the people I am working with. I have learned so much from this one teacher in particular. We work together, brainstorm together, to come up with ways to accomplish our goals."[26]

• *PEP specialists assist evaluators and serve as instructional leaders.* "Our PEP specialist has been really great in trying to explain the whole process, and making it more of our goal, looking at our data."[27] "She [the PEP specialist] did an excellent staff development on goal-setting this year and has conferenced often with lots of teachers to improve instruction."[28]

• *Process enables teachers to be active participants in their evaluation.* "Teachers can take ownership of what they write. They don't have to write a goal based on something that someone is mandating."[29]

• *Emphasizes formative as well as summative evaluation.* "We definitely get an opportunity to suggest through the entire PEP process that there are certain workshops that certain people should attend. We really get a huge opportunity to suggest appropriate staff development."[30]

## Disadvantages

Disadvantages focused on the time demands of academic goal-setting and implementation issues:

• *Can be time-consuming.* "The biggest disadvantage is finding the time to have conversations about the actual work of making the goal happen and meeting with teachers to discuss strategies."[31] "The obstacles are time for administrators, time for teachers; there's never enough time in a day."[32] "If teachers are to engage in the tough work of instructional improvement, the school must organize for it."[33] Goal-setting encourages reflective practice, but time needs to be allocated for it to take place.

• *Student data may be misused or misinterpreted.* "They have us using different children's data to set goals. At the beginning of the year we looked at last year's group's SOL scores. It's helpful in that we can see what we taught well and what we need to improve on, but I think that another piece is that we have to look at data from the group of kids coming to us because they might be weak in other areas."[34] It is critical that schools develop data management systems for making assessment results readily available for teachers to use, both for analyzing student learning patterns from the previous year and identifying the learning needs of incoming students. Even more optimal would be the development of benchmarking tests that some school systems are now beginning to use.[35]

• *Evaluating teachers based on student academic progress can be threatening and increase stress.* "I think part of the fear is that goal-setting and teacher evaluations are going to be linked just to standardized tests. If they did that, then I would not agree with it. I wouldn't want to see standardized test scores be the only measure of my competence as a teacher."[36] Teachers need to be supported in the process of developing goals and have a sense of trust in the constructive purposes of goal-setting.

• *Effectiveness is contingent upon well-trained, accessible PEP specialists.* "You have to have PEP specialists who are qualified, get involved, and know what they are doing in order to do an effective job."[37] "You have to have a PEP specialist who is capable of making sure that teachers understand the importance of the process to their overall teaching assignment."[38]

## What Are the Results of Implementation?

Because academic goal-setting is a work-in-progress for the Alexandria City Public Schools, only preliminary results for this initiative are available at present. At this point, we do know there is a substantial research base for this approach, with its heavy emphasis on identifying the instructional needs of students and focusing teacher effort on these areas.

## What Research Supports a Process Such as Academic Goal-Setting?

Academic goal-setting is closely linked to mastery-learning practices (feedback-corrective teaching), which entails

- Giving students formative tests for the purposes of feedback,
- Providing corrective instructional procedures, and
- Administering additional formative tests to determine the extent to which students have mastered the subject content.

In fact, solid evidence indicates that formative assessment is an essential component to classroom work that can raise student achievement.[39]

Researchers such as Benjamin Bloom have found that students taught under mastery learning achieve, on average, approximately a 1.0 standard deviation above the average of students in conventionally taught classrooms (e.g., 84th percentile vs. 50th percentile).[40]

Academic goal-setting also is linked to enhancing the students' initial cognitive entry prerequisites, which entails

- Developing an initial skills assessment of prerequisites for a course,
- Administering the assessment to students at the beginning of a course, and
- Teaching students specific prerequisites they lack.

Research indicates that, on average, students that are taught the entry prerequisite skills achieve approximately a .7 standard deviation above the average of students in conventionally-taught classrooms (e.g., 76th percentile vs. 50th percentile).[41]

Marzano, Pickering, and Pollock, in their research into research-based strategies for increasing student achievement, reported studies showing percentile gains in student achievement ranging from 18 to 41.[42] Additionally, they drew the following three conclusions from the research on goal-setting:

1. Instructional goals narrow what students focus on. Therefore, while students generally score higher on the instruction related to the specific

academic goal, they likely would score lower (about 8 percentage points) on information that is incidental to the goal, but still covered in the class.

2. Instructional goals should not be too specific. In other words, instructional goals stated in behavioral objective format do not produce student learning gains as high as instructional goals stated in more general formats.

3. Students should be encouraged to personalize the teacher's goals. Once classroom academic goals are set, students should be encouraged to customize them to fit their personal needs.[43]

## Early Perceptions About Academic Goal-Setting

Although it is not possible to present tangible results of the goal-setting process, interviews with internal stakeholders within the Alexandria public school community provided feedback on the perceptions among teachers and administrators (including central office administrators, principals, and program specialists) of academic goal-setting as a component of the teacher evaluation process.

One observation multiple people supported was the pivotal role of the PEP specialists. Simply put, PEP specialists were considered the keystone of the goal-setting process. They were the decisive element in determining whether or not a teacher or administrator felt this program added value to professional development and student learning. Extensive training is necessary to enhance the effectiveness of the specialists because they are responsible for a wide variety of tasks, including staff development regarding instructional strategies, training of teachers in how to appropriately use and interpret student data, and providing continuous support to teachers. The specialists also need to be readily available to assist teachers. Ideally, a PEP specialist should be housed at each school to enhance the effectiveness of the goal-setting process.

## Administrator Perceptions

Administrators note that the goal-setting process is helpful and enables them to identify where teachers require instructional assistance, but acknowledge that the process can increase stress and workloads for teachers. They perceive goal-setting to be an important complement to the other components of the evaluation system that include observation and teacher portfolios. They also view the process as a fair one that places responsibility for success upon the teachers' shoulders. Overall, administrators believe that the goal-setting component of the evaluation process has a significant impact upon teacher instruction and student academic progress.

### Teacher Perceptions

Like the administrators, teachers report that the goal-setting process does help them focus on their students' instructional needs more clearly and adjust instruction accordingly. They also note that the process can increase their stress levels and workloads. Teachers view the goal-setting process as fair as long as the focus remains on professional development and student academic growth. And again like the administrators, teachers believe goal-setting is an important component of the evaluation process, but should be balanced by other elements in the system.

## Conclusion

Although still in its infancy, it is apparent that the Alexandria City Public School system's goal-setting process has the potential to transform how teachers plan and deliver instruction. The assistant superintendent reports that the school system is seeing "a paradigm shift in how teachers and evaluators think about evaluation."[44] We believe the Alexandria public school goal-setting process provides a reasonable way to connect student academic performance and the teacher. Academic goal-setting is linked to mastery learning practices and initial cognitive entry prerequisites, which have been shown to increase student achievement. While goal-setting is only one facet of the comprehensive teacher Performance Evaluation Program, the focus of the overall system is improving the quality of instruction. As reported by Alexandria public school teachers and administrators, the goal-setting process fosters teacher reflection and collegiality, and encourages a collaborative approach to teacher evaluation. Finally, the process encourages teachers to focus on their students' learning needs and make data-driven decisions based upon student data. As one administrator eloquently stated, "The goal really gives us something to shoot for. If we don't get there . . . well, it's kind of like shooting for the stars and landing on the moon. We are moving in a much more positive direction."[45]

# 6

# Assessing Teacher Quality
# Based on Student Gains:
# Value-Added Assessment
# System in Tennessee

*Learning is not attained by chance. It must be sought for
with ardor and attended to with diligence.*
—Abigail Adams

Tennessee has pioneered the use of a statewide approach to measuring student-learning gains, the Tennessee Value-Added Assessment System (TVAAS), which has been in use for more than 10 years. Relying on an extensive database of student records, it provides one of the nation's most systematic analyses of patterns in student achievement.[1] Value-added assessment results are provided by school district, school, and classroom. Although classroom reports are not public, teachers and principals use them to gauge the progress of students within a classroom and to develop professional development goals for teachers. Although the primary purpose of TVAAS is to provide an accountability mechanism for schools and school districts, the teacher effectiveness reports do offer useful feedback for teacher self-assessment and the supervisory process.[2]

TVAAS involves the systematic collection of comparable data on all students across the state annually in the five core subject areas of reading, language, mathematics, science, and social studies. The data are analyzed using a statistical model based on growth, or gains, in student achievement scores rather than fixed standards. Because testing results are collected on every student every year, it is possible to generate useful comparative performance information for the state, school districts, schools, and individual classrooms. The value-added analysis is a multi-step process that generates multiple data points useful for educators and policymakers (see Figure 6.1).[3] Comparisons can be made to any number of possible reference groups to assess whether students are making above-average, average, or below-average progress. This information is invaluable to school leaders at the district and school level in tracking the effects of new initiatives involving curricula, programs, scheduling, and, perhaps most importantly, teachers.

## What Are the Purposes of the Accountability System and How Was It Developed?

TVAAS was adopted as an important centerpiece of a comprehensive Tennessee education reform package, the Education Improvement Act,[4] passed in 1992. It resulted from a court decision that found school funding in Tennessee was inequitable and therefore unconstitutional. In an effort to gain support from the business community to raise the necessary new revenue for schools, the legislature searched for an accountability system that linked student learning to classrooms and schools. Recommendations by William Sanders at the University of Tennessee for a growth model were embraced and incorporated into the original legislation. Subsequently, a mixed-model methodology that Sanders developed was used to support the TVAAS.[5]

Sanders has since achieved prominence for the value-added assessment concept that has been embraced as a potential means of assessing teacher quality.[6] For a number of years, he conducted research on the cumulative and residual effects of instruction on student achievement.[7] In 2000, he retired from the University of Tennessee, where he had directed the Value-Added Research and Assessment Center, and became manager of value-added assessment and research for the SAS Institute, Inc., in Cary, North Carolina.[8] He continues to analyze data for TVAAS and school districts in other states, including Iowa, Ohio, Colorado, and Pennsylvania.[9]

---

**FIGURE 6.1**
**Basic Information Provided by TVAAS***

**Student Level**
- Gains for each subject for the three most recent years
- 3-year average gains
- Comparison of gains to averages for the school, school district, state, and nation

**Teacher Level**
- Average gains of students in each subject and grade level taught by the teacher in the three most recent years
- Average gains of students in the school district in each subject and grade level during the current year
- Comparison of average gains to those for the school district, state, and nation

*The TVAAS database can be used to generate a wide variety of reports based on the needs of the school district, but this example reflects the most commonly used information. In addition, district and state level information is generated but it was not viewed as germane to this discussion of TVAAS' uses.

---

*Source:* Reprinted with permission of the Tennessee Department of Education.

Sanders designed TVAAS to measure the "influence that school systems, schools, and teachers have on indicators of student learning."[10] Using TVAAS as a foundation, the Tennessee legislature set school district performance standards for "demonstrating a mean gain for each academic subject within each grade greater than or equal to the national gain."[11] Also implied in the standards was the expectation that individual teachers would work toward a similar goal within their classrooms. In 1996, this expectation became explicit, and teacher effects on student learning became one of the data sources used for teacher evaluation.[12]

The primary purpose of TVAAS is to satisfy the accountability requirements of the Tennessee Education Improvement Act by providing information on the extent to which teachers, schools, and school systems facilitate learning gains for students as predicted by the previous three-year period. While the TVAAS information is not used as a sole indicator of effectiveness at any level, the information on schools and school systems is made public and creates political pressure for continuous improvement. A clear expectation is that the student achievement data will be used for the development of school and school district improvement plans. At the individual teacher level, the information is *not* public, and is shared only with the teacher and his or her supervisor. It is then used as one data source for the formulation of each teacher's professional growth plan (see Appendix F).

In 1995, the Tennessee State Board of Education called for a re-evaluation of the guidelines for the evaluation of teachers in light of proposed licensure standards, changes in the school improvement planning process, and new initiatives in the state. The Framework for Evaluation and Professional Growth was approved by the board in 1997 and introduced in 2000 to "facilitate the implementation of current initiatives within the state such as the introduction of the Curriculum and Instruction Frameworks and the school improvement process as well as improve the quality of the evaluation process for all teachers."[13] According to the handbook, an emphasis was placed "throughout the evaluation process on developing and assessing the capacity to improve student performance."[14] Figure 6.2 presents one example of how student assessment is integrated into the teacher evaluation process. This chart is part of the Educator Information Record that is shown in Appendix F. An overview of Tennessee's Framework for Evaluation and Professional Growth and the rubrics, or evaluation criteria, for judging the category of "evaluation and assessment" also are found in Appendix F.

A secondary purpose of the TVAAS data, as shown by Figure 6.2, is to serve as a feedback mechanism for curricular planning, program evaluation, and instructional adjustments with students of varying abilities. Test data in the annual reports are disaggregated by subject, grade level, and achievement levels, thereby giving schools information on how program modifications influence student achievement. With the breakdown of testing results by achievement levels, the reports can provide formative information on how modifications have affected all ability levels from low-achieving to high-achieving students. Furthermore, the data offer a measure of the success of educators as well as that of students.[15]

Educational research is yet another purpose of the longitudinal database that TVAAS supports. With millions of records on student achievement across a decade, analyses can be performed to examine the impact of various interventions at different grade levels, in different subjects, and even at

---

**FIGURE 6.2**
**Sample from the Educator Information Record**

Provide one example of pre- and postdata for a class of students. Describe the amount of student progress exhibited and how your conclusions were used to make instructional decisions. (You may attach copies of the assessments.)

| Pre-Instructional Data | Postinstructional Data | Conclusions |
|---|---|---|
|  |  |  |

Use of this Information:

---

*Source:* Reprinted with permission of the Tennessee Department of Education.

different achievement levels. Several research initiatives have been undertaken both in-house and in collaboration with other researchers. One such example has been the examination of the "building change phenomenon,"[16] which has documented the diminished achievement of students in their first year at the next level of schooling (e.g., first year in middle school). Such research has the potential to help educators pinpoint inhibitors to academic growth, and to identify programs or strategies that sustain academic growth to create better learning environments for all students.

As an example, TVAAS data were used in a recent study to examine the effects of restructured schools in Memphis, Tennessee, on student achievement. In 1995, Memphis undertook a major initiative to implement eight different whole-school reform designs in an effort to improve low levels of student learning. With the use of TVAAS data, researchers were able to document greater student gains in restructured schools than non-restructured schools and to determine what reform designs worked better in which schools.[17]

## How Does the Assessment System Work?

The sophisticated statistical methodology of the Tennessee Value-Added Assessment System offers a number of advantages over other approaches that attempt to isolate the effects of schooling on student achievement. The foundation of the system is longitudinal test data collected on every child in the Tennessee public schools. In most cases, several years of test results exist to use in estimating normal learning gains for any given year. Each individual student's previous academic progress then becomes that student's standard for future growth. From a statistical viewpoint, each student's past performance serves as a control for future performance to isolate factors that may affect learning, versus the approach taken by other models in attempting to predict the effects of variables, such as poverty, on achievement.[18]

Beginning in 1993, TVAAS provided compiled data on student academic gains to school systems in the form of a district report. The report summarized student gains for grades 3–8 in the five subjects of reading, language, math, science, and social studies. In addition, data were provided on the predicted growth gains for the district as a whole and average gains for the state and nation. Comparisons were then possible among a number of data points: predicted district gains, actual district gains, and actual state gains.[19]

In that same year, school-level reports providing more narrowly focused school information were issued. Three years later, in 1996, individual teacher reports were distributed for the first time.[20] School-level reports provide data for formative evaluation by detailing the learning gains of students of different achievement levels. According to Sanders and Horn:

> The reports allow school systems to pinpoint grade and subject problems and successes and to direct efforts and resources accordingly. School reports inform principals not only about how effective the 4th-grade math program is, for example, in regard to enhancing student academic gain but also whether it is equally effective in encouraging such growth in its high achievers as well as in its low-achieving students.[21]

Teacher reports contain similar information on average gains and predicted gains for students assigned to that teacher, as well as average gains for the district, state, and nation. At the present time, district, school, and teacher reports are issued on an annual basis. Two sample teacher reports are shown in Figures 6.3 and 6.4. Figure 6.3 is an example of a teacher with "varied effectiveness" who is particularly strong in math and reading, more erratic in language, and weak in social studies and science. Figure 6.4 is an example of a teacher who is "highly effective" in all subjects on a fairly consistent basis across multiple years.

In addition to an analysis of student gains compared to predicted gains, the gain scores of students in a school or school district are compared to national norms. Deviations from the national norm gain are given for each grade and subject, thereby informing schools or districts whether their students are making comparable progress as to other students in the nation. Schools and school districts are expected to achieve the national norm *gains* but not necessarily the national norm *scores*. "The cumulative average gain is the primary indicator by which success is measured,"[22] making growth the consistent focus of analysis.

To support this approach for using student gains as a measure of effectiveness, Sanders and Horn analyzed the cumulative gains for schools across the state. They "found them to be unrelated to the racial composition of schools, the percentage of students receiving free and reduced-price lunches, or the mean achievement level of the school."[23] In other words, factors that are often associated with low achievement levels in absolute terms, such as race and poverty, are not associated with achievement gains. According to one observer, TVAAS has helped shift the focus from absolute achievement levels to learning gains, thereby helping to identify some real heroes in the Tennessee schools who have been overlooked in the past despite the notable learning gains they have made with students.[24] As a corollary, high-achieving students, in absolute terms, have often been found to make minimal year-to-year progress, which is also problematic and a challenge for educators.[25] According to the TVAAS research, the primary predictor of academic growth for students is not prior student achievement level, race, poverty, or class groupings; it is teacher effectiveness.[26]

## Safeguards

Numerous safeguards are built into TVAAS to enhance the fairness of the system:

## FIGURE 6.3
### Sample TVAAS Report Measuring Varied Effectiveness of a Teacher

2002 TVAAS Teacher Report

Teacher: Varied effectiveness
System: Urban School District
School: CCC

Grade: 5

Estimated Mean Gains and (in parentheses) Their Standard Errors

| | Math | | Reading | | Language | | Social Studies | | Science | |
|---|---|---|---|---|---|---|---|---|---|---|
| USA Norm Gain: | 20.0 | | 13.0 | | 15.0 | | 13.0 | | 16.0 | |
| State Mean Gain: | 21.8 | | 14.3 | | 11.9 | | 11.8 | | 18.8 | |
| 2000 Teacher Gain: | 18.6 | (4.1) | 14.4 | (3.6) | 2.6 | (3.7) | 2.8 | (3.6) | 11.2 | (4.0) |
| 2000 System Gain: | 17.7 | (0.3) | 17.0 | (0.3) | 12.3 | (0.3) | 9.8 | (0.3) | 17.0 | (0.3) |
| 2001 Teacher Gain: | 48.7 | (4.1) | 21.8 | (3.4) | 29.2 | (3.7) | 8.2 | (3.6) | 17.4 | (3.9) |
| 2001 System Gain: | 17.1 | (0.3) | 13.8 | (0.2) | 11.8 | (0.3) | 11.7 | (0.3) | 15.6 | (0.3) |
| 2002 Teacher Gain: | 36.9 | (5.0) | 19.5 | (4.3) | 11.9 | (4.2) | 8.7 | (4.9) | 8.8 | (6.3) |
| 2002 System Gain: | 26.1 | (0.3) | 13.7 | (0.2) | 11.5 | (0.3) | 12.1 | (0.3) | 14.8 | (0.3) |
| Teacher 3-Year Average: | 34.7 | (2.5) | 18.6 | (2.2) | 14.6 | (2.2) | 6.6 | (2.4) | 12.5 | (2.8) |
| System 3-Year Average: | 20.3 | (0.2) | 14.8 | (0.1) | 11.9 | (0.2) | 11.2 | (0.2) | 15.8 | (0.2) |

*Teacher 3-Year-Average Gain Comparisons*

| | | | | |
|---|---|---|---|---|
| Teacher v. Norm: | Above Norm | NDD from Norm | Below Norm | NDD from Norm |
| Teacher v. State: | Above Mean | NDD from Mean | Below Mean | Below Mean |
| Teacher v. System: | Above Mean | NDD from Mean | NDD from Mean | NDD from Mean |

Note: NDD = Not Detectably Different (within 2 standard errors)

**Teacher 3-Year-Average Gain in Scale Score Units with Approximate 95% Confidence Intervals**

```
                0         10        20        30        40        50
                +....+....+....+....+....+....+....+....+....+....+....+
Math                              N  SL_--T-----)
Reading                        (-.-*--TN---)               (-----T-----)
Language           (-----T-----LS N
Social Studies     (-----T---LN--) S
Science                                       NL S
```

Legend: T = Teacher Gain, L = System (LEA) Mean Gain, S = State Mean Gain, N = National Norm Gain
An asterisk (*) indicates that 2 or more of the above symbols coincide.

The estimated teacher gains presented here are the official TVAAS estimates from the statistical mixed model methodology that protects each teacher from misleading results due to random occurrences. Each teacher's gain is assumed to be equal to the average gain for the district until the weight of the data pulls the estimate away from the district average. This year's estimates of previous years' gains may have changed as a result of incorporating the most recent student data.

*Source:* Report provided by William Sanders. Reprinted with permission.

**FIGURE 6.4**

**Sample TVAAS Report of a Highly Effective Teacher**

2002 TVAAS Teacher Report

Teacher: Highly Effective Teacher
System: Urban School District
School: AAA

Grade: 5

Estimated Mean Gains and (in parentheses) Their Standard Errors

| | Math | Reading | Language | Social Studies | Science |
|---|---|---|---|---|---|
| USA Norm Gain: | 20.0 | 13.0 | 15.0 | 13.0 | 16.0 |
| State Mean Gain: | 21.8 | 14.3 | 11.9 | 11.8 | 18.8 |
| 2000 Teacher Gain: | 8.6 (3.6) | 18.5 (2.9) | 15.7 (3.0) | 9.3 (2.9) | 6.6 (3.9) |
| 2000 System Gain: | 17.7 (0.3) | 17.0 (0.3) | 12.3 (0.3) | 9.8 (0.3) | 17.0 (0.3) |
| 2001 Teacher Gain: | 29.5 (4.0) | 22.8 (3.2) | 19.8 (3.5) | 14.1 (3.1) | 16.4 (4.1) |
| 2001 System Gain: | 17.1 (0.3) | 13.8 (0.2) | 11.8 (0.3) | 11.7 (0.3) | 15.6 (0.3) |
| 2002 Teacher Gain: | 59.3 (4.8) | 23.6 (3.6) | 30.5 (4.0) | 21.9 (4.1) | 40.4 (5.0) |
| 2002 System Gain: | 26.1 (0.3) | 13.7 (0.2) | 11.5 (0.3) | 12.1 (0.3) | 14.8 (0.3) |
| Teacher 3-Year Average: | 32.3 (2.4) | 21.6 (1.9) | 22.0 (2.0) | 15.1 (2.0) | 21.1 (2.5) |
| System 3-Year Average: | 20.3 (0.2) | 14.8 (0.1) | 11.9 (0.2) | 11.2 (0.2) | 15.8 (0.2) |

*Teacher 3-Year-Average Gain Comparisons*

| | | | | |
|---|---|---|---|---|
| Teacher v. Norm: | Above Norm | Above Norm | NDD from Norm | Above Norm | Above Norm |
| Teacher v. State: | Above Mean | Above Mean | NDD from Mean | NDD from Mean | Above Mean |
| Teacher v. System: | Above Mean | Above Mean | NDD from Mean | NDD from Mean | Below Mean |

Note: NDD = Not Detectably Different (within 2 standard errors)

**Teacher 3-Year-Average Gain in Scale Score Units with Approximate 95% Confidence Intervals**

```
                0         10        20        30        40        50
                + ....... + ....... + ....... + ....... + ....... +
Math                            NL S    ( - - - - - T - - - - - )
Reading                   N  SL   ( - - - T - - - )
Language              *  N   ( - - - - T - - - )
Social Studies     LS-N - - T - - - - )
Science                LN - - - S - - - T - - - - )
```

Legend: T = Teacher Gain, L = System (LEA) Mean Gain, S = State Mean Gain, N = National Norm Gain
An asterisk (*) indicates that 2 or more of the above symbols coincide.

The estimated teacher gains presented here are the official TVAAS estimates from the statistical mixed model methodology that protects each teacher from misleading results due to random occurrences. Each teacher's gain is assumed to be equal to the average gain for the district until the weight of the data pulls the estimate away from the district average. This year's estimates of previous years' gains may have changed as a result of incorporating the most recent student data.

*Source:* Report provided by William Sanders. Reprinted with permission.

- Estimates of school, school system, and teacher effectiveness are based on at least three years and no more than five years of assessment data to ensure statistical stability.[27]

- Schools, school systems, and teachers cannot be assessed solely on the basis of TVAAS.[28]

- A variety of media have helped develop an understanding among educators about how to interpret and use TVAAS, including booklets, reports, workshops, presentations, and video presentations.

- A "shrinkage" estimate is a statistical methodology used to ensure accurate estimates of the effects of a teacher, school, or school system on student gain. For teachers, this means, "all teachers are assumed to be the average of their school system until the weight of the data pulls their specific estimates away from their school system's mean."[29] This kind of tool protects teachers, schools, and school districts from short-term fluctuations in the test results or other aberrations in data analysis that would misrepresent actual results.

- "Students must be tested annually with fresh, equivalent, non-redundant tests that exhibit a high level of reliability and validity."[30] Doing so ensures that tests are comparable statistically year to year but the specific items vary so that "teaching to the test" is minimized.[31]

- Students identified by the school-based special education teams are excluded from the analysis of teacher effects. However, virtually no students are excluded from the analysis of school effects.

- Students are not included in a teacher's assessment data unless they have been present 150 days in a given school year.[32]

- Test security is a high priority, with stringent sanctions for impropriety. TVAAS is also designed to "kick out" suspicious data.[33]

- Estimates of the impact of poverty, limited English proficiency, parents' level of education, and other variables are unnecessary because they remain relatively constant for each child from year to year.

## What Are the Student Assessment Strategies?

TVAAS uses data from an existing statewide testing program. It could, however, use other types of data if instrumentation was developed. The primary assessment instruments that Tennessee currently uses include

- The Tennessee Comprehensive Assessment Program for grades 3–8 in the subject areas of science, math, social studies, language arts, and reading;[34]
- End-of-course tests in high school subjects that count toward the course grade; and
- A writing assessment in grades 5, 8, and 11.[35]

The Tennessee Comprehensive Assessment Program (TCAP) is a combination of norm-referenced items from TerraNova[36] and criterion-referenced items selected by teachers to reflect closely the Tennessee curricula. A high correlation is found between the norm-referenced and criterion-referenced items. Currently, end-of-course tests are being developed in the major subject areas for grades 9–12.

Using the Tennessee Comprehensive Assessment Program data, the following basic steps are taken to make the testing information useful:

1. Determine the *improvement* or gain in test scores for each subject for each student.

2. Compare the students' *actual* gain to the *expected* gain based on their past performance.

3. Compile individual student gains at the class, school, district, and state levels.

4. Compare aggregated data to average gains for the school, district, state, and nation.

## How Is the Assessment System Related to Teacher Evaluation?

The Education Improvement Act requires TVAAS data to be used when evaluating teachers for whom it is available, but it cannot be the sole source of information. Based on the Framework for Evaluation and Professional Growth, teachers work with their principals to develop a professional development plan, linked to the school's improvement plan and reflective of the data from the TVAAS teacher report. Teacher reports provide useful diagnostic information for improving instruction based on curriculum-aligned assessments. Other options for teacher evaluation include (1) cognitive coaching, (2) teacher-devised professional improvement plans, (3) cooperative teaching-related projects, and (4) classroom observations.[37]

The emphasis on the outcomes of teaching is clear in the Framework for Evaluation and Professional Growth. According to the manual, it "was designed to provide for an evaluation process, which requires the examination of

- What students need to know and be able to do.
- What the teacher has been doing to effect this learning.
- The degree of student success in achieving those objectives.
- The implications for continuing employment and future professional [growth]."[38]

## What Are the Advantages and Disadvantages of the Assessment System?

The TVAAS is a carefully conceptualized, highly technical statistical approach to measuring student gains. The resulting longitudinal database provides an excellent research tool and useful data for examining teacher and school effects on student learning. Given its reliance on paper and pencil tests, however, reservations remain about its use for evaluation purposes. The following are some of the specific strengths and weaknesses.

### Advantages

Advantages include the strong statistical properties of TVAAS and its focus on improvement or gains in student achievement:

- *TVAAS is based on sophisticated statistical models that are capable of handling years of longitudinal student achievement data.*[39] Unlike most state-level databases, the Tennessee model tracks students through their years of school, linking their scale scores and calculating gains at the individual level, which are then aggregated at the classroom, school, district, and state levels.
- *TVAAS is viewed by statistical experts as robust, fair, reliable, and valid.*[40] According to a review of TVAAS by Walberg and Paik, "particularly strong points of TVAAS are the analysis of several years of data on teachers and an apparent system robustness despite ubiquitous missing data problems in longitudinal records."[41]
- *With a focus on improvement instead of achievement based on fixed standards, individual differences are accommodated.* Students are expected to grow

and improve but not necessarily at the same rate or reaching the same goal at the same time as other students. In some schools, math students are regrouped frequently to better focus instruction on weaker skills or concepts. Teachers see many of these changes as positive. They now "accept kids where they are and then take them as far as possible."[42]

• *Teacher data provide a relatively simple measure of student progress and a teacher's ability to influence student learning outcomes.* Teachers acknowledge that TVAAS is one part of an effort to give the public some measure of their accomplishments and to make the schools as effective as possible. Although they found it overwhelming at first, they are developing a comfort level as well as a sense that the system can be a positive tool. [43]

• *TCAP has good content validity because of the high degree of alignment with the Tennessee curricula.*[44] The Tennessee Comprehensive Assessment Program achievement tests actually contain both norm-referenced items and criterion-referenced items that match the Tennessee curricula. There is also a high correlation between the criterion-referenced items and the norm-referenced items.[45]

• *Researchers have found a positive correlation between teacher effects as determined by TVAAS and subjective evaluations by supervisors.* Research conducted as part of a feasibility study for TVAAS found a moderate relationship between quantitative measures of student gains and clinical judgments of their supervisors.[46]

## Disadvantages

The major disadvantages noted for TVAAS are due in part to its sophistication and concerns about testing in general:

• *TVAAS involves sophisticated statistical analyses that require a substantial programming effort and computing capability.* The University of Tennessee Value-Added Research and Assessment Center originally developed the software to handle the mixed-model application for this large database. The center processed the information on a "UNIX workstation with 1 gigabyte of physical memory and 13 gigabytes of hard disk storage."[47] Today the SAS Institute in North Carolina processes the data for Tennessee and a number of other states. The statistical expertise and computing power to undertake an effort of this complexity is a possible challenge to many users.

• *The TVAAS model assumes that students are randomly distributed in classrooms and schools.* In reality, this is not the case. Evidence suggests that low-SES students not only begin at lower levels of performance but also progress at a slower rate. Larger numbers of low-SES students would produce lower gains and unfairly depict the efforts of even the most accomplished teachers.[48]

 • *Potential exists for misuse or misinterpretation of data.* Concerns exist about the over-reliance on TVAAS as a sole, or even primary, indicator of success in teacher evaluation; the lack of training for administrators in its use and interpretation; and the narrow ability of TVAAS to measure the breadth of the enterprise called learning. Variation is found in how different principals use the information, both positively and negatively.[49] In some cases, teachers noted that principals misused the data and unfairly blamed teachers for poor results. A number of interviewed educators confirmed that test results have been used as a basis for remediation and reassignment, but not for teacher dismissal.[50]

 • *Annual testing of students is a major investment of time, money, and human effort.* Concerns also exist that the benefits don't justify the costs and that a comparable investment in professional development would be a better use of the money.[51] The actual cost of TVAAS in 1995 was 60 cents per student and TCAP was $3.59 per student. The combined cost of TVAAS and TCAP was less than one percent of the 1995 per-pupil expenditures for students in Tennessee.[52]

 • *TCAP provides a limited measure of the complex purposes of education.* According to critics like Linda Darling-Hammond, it is questionable "what multiple-choice responses really measure . . . and they give no indication of the ability to apply information in a performance context."[53]

 • *TVAAS findings have not been adequately verified by independent researchers.* Some researchers question the validity of the statistical methodology and recommend further inquiry before there is widespread implementation.[54] However, an independent evaluation of TVAAS by the Tennessee Comptroller of the Treasury found that estimates of teacher gain effects were stable and able to distinguish poor and exceptional teacher effectiveness.[55] But, additional research needs to be conducted on the design and application of TVAAS.

To his credit, Sanders has continued to develop the methodology that supports TVAAS, and acknowledges the limitations of the system: "There is no way you can measure all of the important things a teacher does in the classroom. But that doesn't mean you shouldn't be measuring the things that can be measured."[56]

## What Are the Results of Implementation?

The impact of TVAAS on student learning is of primary importance. Tennessee has been able to document increased student achievement for 8th grade students who were in school and tested from 1991–97, the time frame during which TVAAS was first implemented.[57] During those years, average student achievement as measured by TVAAS increased in math, science, and language; however, social studies remained constant and reading decreased slightly (2 scale score points). The 2003 TVAAS reports show that the state 3-year-average gains and mean scale scores in math exceed the national norms at every tested grade level except one, but results are mixed in reading.[58] National Assessment of Educational Progress (NAEP) data for the years 1992–2003 indicate increases in 4th and 8th grade math scores that closely track national averages. Reading scores have remained flat during the same timeframe but are consistent with national averages.[59] Overall, Tennessee was able to make some early gains in math when TVAAS was introduced, and has been able to maintain a student achievement record that closely mirrors that of the nation based on NAEP data.

Another area of impact has been in providing a focus for staff development. Test data are used to identify areas of insufficient instruction so that curricula or instructional strategies can be modified (e.g., in writing). Based on the results of test data, intensive staff development has occurred in this area, with teachers reporting both subjective and objective measures of improvement. Many teachers seek out colleagues who have been highly effective in teaching the curriculum for ideas and suggestions. These teachers are sharing their work with colleagues through observations and workshops. For example, the statewide Title I conference has served as a forum for presentations by teachers who have been particularly effective in enhancing student performance.[60]

More recently, Tennessee has proposed using the TVAAS teacher reports as one means of demonstrating that teachers are "highly qualified" under the No Child Left Behind legislation. The selection of TVAAS data to substantiate competence would be a voluntary choice by the teacher, and the test-score information would remain confidential. This 3-year average gain data would meet the "high, objective, uniform state standard of evaluation" or HOUSE requirement of the federal regulations, and the concept seems to be supported by both the U.S. Department of Education and the Tennessee Education Association.[61]

Another innovative use of the TVAAS data has been to identify high-performing teachers in Chattanooga, Tennessee, to work in the district's most challenging schools. Along with portfolios of student work and lesson plans, TVAAS test data have been used to identify teachers with the instructional skills that the system's nine lowest-scoring schools need. These teachers are paid an extra $5000 per year to teach in the low-performing schools, although for most, the recognition and challenge were the reasons they chose to make the move. In addition to the recruitment of talented teachers, the leadership was changed at two-thirds of the schools, some teachers were removed, additional teacher training was provided, the use of data was emphasized to inform instruction, and financial incentives were offered to retain the strong teachers already in the schools. After two years of implementation, increases of 10 percentile points have occurred among 3rd graders reading at or above grade level.[62]

Despite these successful uses of TVAAS, universal support for the system does not exist. In fact, two bills that would eliminate it were introduced in the Tennessee legislature during the 2004 session. Two legislators from Nashville introduced the measures in response to concerns by the Nashville public schools regarding discrepancies between raw scores and value-added measures. The legislative liaison for the Tennessee Department of Education suggested that the concerns of the legislators needed to be addressed.[63] Meanwhile, Kevin Carey at the Education Trust, in a recent issue of *Thinking K–16*, described TVAAS as "easily the best example" of a model to measure teacher effectiveness. TVAAS remains controversial, but detractors seem to be outnumbered by endorsers.[64]

## Teacher Perspectives

Teachers interviewed in Tennessee acknowledged that the TVAAS results add pressure to the job, but "it keeps you on your toes." Both advocates and skeptics abound regarding the use of TVAAS for measuring student learning. One teacher shared that with TVAAS, "one can't blame anyone else for student progress or lack thereof; it's the teacher's responsibility."[65] It motivated her to stop and examine her practice. She found that she did not sufficiently review material with students to maintain mastery; with minor changes in her instruction, students were able to demonstrate substantial gains in their yearly achievement.[66] Other teachers remain skeptical or highly critical of the system and hope that it will go away.[67]

In terms of instruction, interviewed teachers stated that they now teach at a higher level in all subject areas and concentrate the teaching in a more curriculum-focused manner. One teacher reported, "There is not a lot of fluff, it is direct teaching all day long."[68] Another change teachers noted has been in science, with increased emphasis on hands-on activities to foster problem-solving skills reflected in the science curriculum and the TCAP test items. Based on this limited sample of teachers, it is unclear how teachers in general view TVAAS, but some do perceive it as a means to improve their instruction.[69]

### Principal Perspectives

TVAAS provides school- and teacher-based data that some principals find useful for school improvement. "Once you recognize what data does for you, if you've got the philosophy and willingness to change the school, you can drastically affect the learning of individual students. It's that simple."[70] Another principal noted that the information enhances data-driven decision-making, which yields good gains and a sense of school pride. The feedback helps to focus everyone on achievement and improves performance.

Rick Privette, former principal at Carver Elementary School in East Knox County, said that he tried to make the sharing of TVAAS data with teachers non-threatening, and he balanced it with professional judgment. He examined the data for patterns of results and, if necessary, addressed needed improvements in the annual development plan. He emphasized that test results were not used as the sole means of teacher evaluation.[71]

## Conclusion

The developers of TVAAS have expressed the goal of providing educators with information that will foster direction for improving student academic gains, thereby enabling students to receive more equal opportunities regardless of where they go to school.[72] Sanders said that "we hope our research is used for diagnostic purposes so teachers can consider what they're doing and how to improve it."[73] Properly conducted and analyzed, test results have the potential to provide one set of lenses for making sense of the effects of schooling and, in particular, teaching on student learning. Results from TVAAS suggest that students in Tennessee are doing better on TCAP, and teachers report more focused instruction in classrooms.

As schools and policy makers pursue progressively better approaches to ensuring quality education for all students, TVAAS distinguishes itself by shifting the focus from fixed standards to academic progress and truly individualizes discussions of student progress. Sanders and Horn spoke of these moral obligations to students when they stated:

> TVAAS was developed on the premise that society has a right to expect that schools will provide students with the opportunity for academic gain regardless of the level at which the students enter the educational venue. In other words, all students can and should learn commensurate with their abilities.[74]

TVAAS data provide important feedback on the learning process and inform the teacher evaluation process in a systematic and reliable manner. When the data are used in the proper context, as only one source of information, they have tremendous potential to inform the practice of teaching and enhance student achievement.

# 7

# Final Thoughts on Assessing Teacher Quality: Guidelines for Policy and Practice

*Who dares to teach must never cease to learn.*

—John Cotton Dana

Over the past two decades, the standards movement has swept the country, state-by-state, and has now culminated in No Child Left Behind at the federal level. Despite the controversy surrounding both standards and the federal legislation, the framework for how we think about education has been changed forever. Standards have defined tangible goals for the educational enterprise, not only *what* will be learned but by *whom* and *how well*. Educators in most states now have specific expectations for what students should know and be able to do after a year of instruction and are accountable for those results. Better defined goals have shifted the educational dialogue from vague opinions about student progress to factual evidence of student performance.

The testing information that provides data on goal attainment at the school and school district levels also can be used at the classroom level for assessing teacher quality. For most school districts, classroom observation continues to be the traditional approach to teacher evaluation, despite the fact that observations and judgments about what teachers *do* in the class-room are a poor proxy for what they actually *accomplish* with individual students. Somehow we have come to believe that the observation of one class period is indicative of what teachers do during the other thousand hours they teach in a given year. Moreover, we seem to think that supervisors can infer what students do or do not learn from observing a teaching episode. Student assessment data have the potential to transform teacher evaluation from one of *opinions* about professional ability to one of *factual information* on what teachers actually accomplish with students.

We have presented four relatively distinct models that support this shift in how we assess teacher quality. Drawing from the four case studies presented in the previous chapters, we have examined and critiqued a range of possible strategies that measure student learning and link it to the assessment of teachers. The possibilities fall on a continuum from a highly individualized and qualitative approach with the Oregon Work Sample Methodology to a sophisticated statistical approach with the Tennessee Value-Added Assessment System. In this final chapter, first we briefly examine lessons learned from using measures of student learning in teacher assessment, including potential benefits and drawbacks. Then, we offer a set of specific recommendations to guide the use of student assessment in teacher evaluation.

## Lessons Learned About Using Measures of Student Learning

In Tennessee, where gain scores on standardized achievement tests have been used, student achievement levels have increased. Test results have informed teacher evaluation and guided improvement assistance. They are used as one data point, along with more clinical approaches, in evaluation. In Oregon; Alexandria, Virginia; and Loveland, Colorado, where the impact of teacher performance on student learning has been documented with more of a mixed design using both qualitative and quantitative measures, the promise and evidence for focused teacher efforts and improved student learning also exist. In the Oregon Work Sample Methodology, actual samples of teacher work are assessed for their connection to classroom-based student learning. In the Alexandria and Thompson school districts, teacher job performance standards are connected directly to student learning, using both classroom indices and standardized tests as measures of student learning. Figure 7.1 summarizes the key features from the four teacher assessment systems.

In all four of the case studies presented in this book, test data are used to some extent as one element of multiple measures for assessing teacher effectiveness and are used to focus professional development, often on issues of practice and what works to enhance learning for children. Teachers who have been more successful in achieving high student performance have been identified and encouraged to share their instructional strategies. Moreover, in each of these teacher assessment systems the integration of student learning into teacher assessment is designed to foster both formative and summative teacher assessment and, ultimately, increased student learning.

Student assessment measures are a source of information that can be used to diagnostically enhance instruction and services at the classroom, school, or program level. Additionally, they can help evaluate the effectiveness of various interventions on different groups of students. If thoughtfully used, student assessment data truly can "guide investments in school and teacher learning [that are] linked to changes in practice," as suggested by Linda Darling-Hammond.[1] In response to better identified shortcomings in the current use of resources, schools are beginning to experiment with regrouping, more structured diagnostic assessments, different uses of time for different children, and better articulation of the curriculum. The use of student assessment information can inform research on the impact of these reform efforts, can confirm anecdotal reports of success, and explore the unintended consequences.

As we attempt to link student learning with teacher effectiveness, it is important to remember that tests and other types of student assessments have the potential for benefit or misuse. But, as educators we must actively embrace the possibilities of using student achievement measures as a tool, one of many, to make education more meaningful and productive for students of all ability levels.

## Basic Requirements of Fair Testing Programs That Inform Teacher Evaluation

If student learning is the stated objective of schooling,[2] then it is only reasonable that we consider some measure or indication of student learning in

## FIGURE 7.1
### Implications for Using Student Learning Measures
### in Teacher Quality Assessment

| Practice | Oregon: Work Sample Methodology Model | Thompson School District (Colo.): Standards Based Model |
|---|---|---|
| Student Learning | The TWSM is an authentic and applied appraisal system that is designed to portray student-learning progress as "outcomes desired by a teacher and taught by a teacher." | The system is designed to increase "the probability of advancing student learning" as measured by various standardized achievement tests. Student learning has improved. |
| Instructional Assistance for Students | Because of the "action research" nature of the TWSM, a key benefit is early and direct classroom instructional assistance for individual students and students clustered by learning needs. | The system encourages teachers to focus on individual student learning needs through content standards, learning styles, teaching/learning strategies, and assessment of learning results. |
| Personnel Actions | To date, The Oregon TWSM has been used in initial teacher licensure. It has proven to be a viable tool for screening candidates for entry into the teaching profession. | Teacher performance standards are clearly delineated, assessed partially on student learning, and then tied to professional development. The focus of the system is on performance assistance and improvement. |
| Professional Development | The TWSM is designed to foster both formative and summative teacher reflection and self-evaluation. | The results of the evaluation cycle for each teacher are connected to professional development needs in the teachers in achieving their upcoming evaluation cycle. |

| Alexandria School District (Va.): Student Academic Goal-Setting Model | Tennessee: Value-Added Assessment System |
| --- | --- |
| The purpose of the model is to foster reflection on student needs as a basic component of evaluation and professional development. (Still in the piloting stage.) | Increased student achievement has been documented in math, science, and language, with reading and social studies remaining relatively constant. |
| The goal-setting process focuses teacher efforts on the specific instructional needs of students. One of its purposes is to shift the focus from content-centered to student-centered instruction. | Emphasis has been on teaching the curriculum more thoroughly with built-in reviews. Students are regrouped more frequently to focus instruction on weaker skills or concepts. |
| The goal-setting process is an integral part of the overall teacher evaluation system, and there is additional pressure to improve student learning, though the focus is on professional development. | Test results are one source of data but cannot be the sole source of information for evaluation. They are used for remediation when needed. |
| The PEP specialists work with teachers individually to both develop student learning goals and offer resources to support the goals. | Professional development needs, as reflected in summative teacher evaluations, are left to the discretion of the local school. |

assessing teacher quality. Unfortunately, most ratings of teacher effectiveness bear little relationship to measures of pupil achievement. Although we readily acknowledge the potential pitfalls of making this connection, as well as the need for additional research in this arena, we have found ample evidence to suggest that there are ways to make the connection in a thoughtful and constructive manner that benefits children.

First and foremost, when student learning measures are used in the evaluation of teachers and other educators, they must conform to professional standards of practice.[3] While numerous pitfalls exist with the unschooled use of assessment data for evaluation of any sort, particularly for use in performance evaluation, it is important to maximize the benefits and minimize the liabilities in linking student learning and teacher effectiveness. Therefore, we propose several practices to reduce possible bias and increase the fairness of using student assessment data in teacher assessment.

### 1. Use student learning as *only one* component of a teacher assessment system that is based on multiple data sources.

We maintain that measures of student learning are vitally important to judging the effectiveness of teachers and schools, but should never usurp professional judgment that integrates knowledge of other factors that affect instruction, such as the lack of resources, overcrowding, and community poverty. Teaching and learning are far too complex to be reduced to a single test result or even a battery of tests. Tests, however, can serve as indicators of other problems in specific classrooms or schools that need to be addressed through staff development, teacher mentoring, greater resources, or reorganization of time and curriculum.

As discussed in Chapter 2, we advocate the use of test results in teacher evaluation as a complement to traditional supervision based on classroom observations and other pertinent data sources. Supervision provides information on the *act* of teaching: the decisions that are made in the selection, organization, and delivery of instruction. Test results provide information on the *results* of teaching. Evaluation of the means seems meaningless without some gauge of the ends. But on the other hand, the ends can never justify questionable means. A balanced approach to evaluation would consider both by using multiple measures.

## 2. Consider the context in which teaching and learning occur.

The Tennessee Value-Added Assessment System studies report that "the two most important factors impacting student gain are the teacher and the achievement level for the student [e.g., how much students had achieved prior to coming to a given classroom]."[4] Moreover, the studies provide evidence that teacher effectiveness is a far more powerful determinant of student learning than selected contextual variables. The researchers concluded that:

> Differences in teacher effectiveness were found to be the dominant factor affecting student academic gain. The importance of the effects of certain classroom contextual variables (class size and classroom heterogeneity) appears to be minor and should not be viewed as inhibitors to the appropriate use of student outcome data in teacher assessment.[5]

Despite these findings, we contend that circumstances occur where teachers have done everything possible at the classroom level to enhance instruction, but that conditions beyond their control, such as unreasonably large class sizes or classes taught without a complete set of textbooks, prevent maximum benefit by children. Consequently, we recommend that consideration be given for real impediments to student learning, such as student mobility, absenteeism, and other variables beyond the control of the teacher. The whole system of support, including staff training, availability of mentors, conducive workspaces, books, and instructional materials cannot be overlooked in attributing responsibility for learning. Until teachers teach in fully supportive environments, these circumstances must be taken into account.

## 3. Use measures of student growth versus fixed achievement standards or goals.

In the real world, very few human endeavors are judged in terms of fixed goals; more typically, they are based on growth and progress toward stated goals. Even the hard-nosed world of business judges performance based on a variety of economic indicators and comparisons to projected growth. We propose that the same paradigm be used in education with an acknowledgment of learning inhibitors and comparisons to projected learning growth. This approach requires the use of pre- and post-testing to determine progress versus the attainment of predetermined pass rates or proficiency levels. While there is a place and purpose for fixed standards, such as learning to read at an acceptable level, fixed standards must be regarded skeptically when applied to personnel evaluation. It is one thing to expect teachers to help students learn and improve their skills; it is quite different to expect them to transport all incoming students, no matter what their skill level, to the exact same destination in one year.

When student learning is communicated in terms of absolute achievement (e.g., 70 percent correct on reading comprehension), it perpetuates a meritocracy of the "haves" and the "have-nots." As James Popham observed,[6] absolute achievement scores tend to reflect what children bring to school, not necessarily what they have learned in school. Absolute achievement scores also tend to preserve the notion that it is aptitude that counts in school and not effort. Not only is this counterproductive for students of all ability levels, it also renders teachers irrelevant in the educational process if we simply attribute success to the ability of students when they walk into school. If student learning is truly our goal in schools, we must create environments for effort-based learning as described by Lauren Resnick,[7] with the focus on achievement growth. True measures of learning should focus on growth in knowledge and skills, not on student aptitude.

The use of absolute achievement scores also penalizes the teachers and schools who work with the least prepared and most challenging learners. When you begin with a high-achieving group, "good" test results are a foregone conclusion and vice versa. What is the incentive for students, teachers, or schools to invest a great deal of effort in learning when the goal is preordained? Our most effective teachers are those who take all students from where they are academically and creatively respond to their learning needs and interests. Effective teachers move students forward and assist them in achieving definable academic goals, whether they begin with weak or strong academic skills.

Pre- and post-testing in a specific subject area during a given year can be used to generate a gain score, as was discussed in the chapters on the Thompson, Colorado, model and the Tennessee Value-Added Assessment System. We believe this shift to an emphasis on growth is critical, but the Tennessee model takes this concept a step further by comparing a student's *actual* growth, using the gain score, to her *projected* growth, based on three years of prior achievement. In this way, judgments can be made about the effectiveness of current instruction as compared to that in previous years.

## 4. Compare learning gains from one point in time to another for the same students, not different groups of students.

Implicit in the concept of gain scores is the assumption that similar tests will be used to measure student learning across time on an individual basis. When student learning is aggregated across a class of students, we believe a reasonably fair measure of teacher effects is generated. Teacher effects are not gauged in a fair manner when the absolute achievement level of one class of students is compared to the absolute achievement of a different class of students. Although this is common practice at the school and school district level, it is unfair and unreasonable at the individual teacher level. It holds teachers accountable for the performance of two different groups of students with potentially discrepant sets of prerequisite knowledge and skills. This type of comparison invites the type of bias that gain scores were intended to minimize.

## 5. Recognize that gain scores have pitfalls that must be avoided.

Even when measures of student growth are used, properly interpreting gain scores is critical. In particular, a statistical artifact known as the regression effect needs to be considered. It results in a tendency for students starting with low performance levels to show larger gains than warranted. Conversely, because of a ceiling effect, students who start with high performance may show lower gains, or even declines, if the measure of achievement is not adequately difficult to gauge what those high-scoring students actually know and are able to do.[8]

## 6. Use a timeframe for teacher assessment that allows for patterns of student learning to be documented in a fair manner.

If teachers are to be held accountable for student learning, then it is critical that patterns of student learning be established, not single snapshots. We support the suggestion by Sanders and his colleagues "that teacher evaluation processes should include, as a major component, a reliable and valid measure of a teacher's effect on student academic growth over time. The use of student achievement data from an appropriately drawn standardized testing program administered longitudinally and appropriately analyzed can fulfill these requirements."[9]

Repeated measures of student learning over time enhance reliability from a statistical point of view and credibility from a decision-making perspective. The scoring errors made by CTB/McGraw-Hill in 1998–99 emphasize the serious consequences of placing too much credence on a single set of test results.[10] The test results for students in six states were compromised by the errors. In New York City alone, more than 8,000 students were required to attend summer school based on low test scores that were incorrect. In contrast, Tennessee, which had longitudinal data on most of its students, was able to flag the errors in the testing reports before they were distributed to schools and students.[11] They delayed critical decision-making until they had corrected test results, thereby demonstrating the power of multiple measures of student learning.

## 7. Use fair and valid measures of student learning.

Reliability, validity, freedom from bias, and fairness are obvious concerns and conditions for connecting student assessment to teacher assessment. Drawing on the work of Wheeler,[12] McConney, Schalock, and Schalock,[13] and others,[14] we propose several practices to increase the fairness of using student assessment data in the evaluation of educational personnel. Specifically, the use of student assessment measures in assessing teacher performance should be:

- *Valid:* "Any measure of student performance, whether used for formative or summative evaluation, should be sensitive to (be able to detect) the impacts of what teachers and schools do; that is, measures of student learning should have instructional validity. If they do not . . . then it would be hard to justify their use for either teacher or school evaluation of any kind."[15]

- *Reliable:* The assessment measure should produce adequately consistent (e.g., reliable) results across time and across scorers.[16] One of the key issues to consider when making decisions about teacher performance is interrater reliability among evaluators.

- *Free from bias:* Student achievement data should be used in an objective, fair, and impartial manner, and should not be interpreted or used capriciously.

• *Comparable*: Results for one teacher should be comparable to results for other teachers. "No teacher . . . should be disadvantaged compared with any other based on factors beyond their control."[17]

## 8. Select student assessment measures that are most closely aligned with existing curricula.

Given that no national curriculum standards exist, test makers must select the content for inclusion on standardized tests and other measures of student performance. Their selections may or may not reflect state or local curricula. Some states have contracted for the development of customized tests that reflect the state-mandated curriculum, but even then there can be incongruencies with delivery of the curriculum in different school districts, schools, and classrooms. Standardized tests will never be perfectly aligned with delivered curricula; only the classroom teacher can ensure that level of alignment, which supports the need for a variety of assessment strategies. However, standardized tests should be selected based on their general or predominant alignment with the articulated curriculum.

When standardized measures of student achievement are selected without regard to the curriculum, they do not fairly reflect teaching or learning except in a very general sense. They may reflect a general body of knowledge and skills acquired in school or at home, but they do not reflect specific instruction by a particular teacher during a precise period of time. If student assessment measures are unrelated to what has been taught, then they cannot be used to measure the impact of teaching:

> Any measure of student performance, whether used for formative or summative teacher or school evaluation, should be consistent with the curricula of courses, programs, and/or schools. The measures should reflect both the scope and complexity of the content taught. If they do not, then it would be hard to defend the claim that a full and representative sample of teachers' or schools' work is reflected by student performance data. Worse, it may be that the student performance measures assess content that *is not* part of the curricula of courses, programs, and/or schools. This would be akin to holding teachers and schools accountable for outcomes for which they are not responsible.[18]

Tests that are disconnected from curricula may provide a gauge of what students know compared to other students in the same grade across the nation, but they hardly provide a basis for judging teaching effectiveness. The value of student assessment measures for educators is proportional to their alignment with the curriculum. Therefore, student achievement measures used in teacher assessment must have sufficient curriculum validity.

### 9. Don't narrow the curriculum and limit teaching to fit a test unless the test actually measures what should be taught.

Another unintended but predictable consequence of selecting standardized tests that are not aligned with the curriculum is the distortion of the curriculum to meet the demands of the test. A basic educational principle is the purposeful alignment of curriculum, instruction, and assessment. Ideally, curriculum and instruction drive assessment, but if assessment is fixed and used for high-stakes decisions, then it can drive the curriculum and instruction. This is a subversion of the educational process, and it allows tests and test makers to determine the content and pacing of teaching. No one intends for this to happen, but evidence abounds that it occurs and that it is one of the reasons many teachers object to testing programs. Based on a standard of fairness, this concern seems justified.

## Conclusion

If any lesson is to be learned from these chapters, it is that teachers make a difference in student learning. Given the clear and undeniable link that exists between teacher effectiveness and student learning, we support the use of student achievement information in teacher assessment. Student achievement can, and indeed should, be an important source of feedback on the effectiveness of schools, administrators, and teachers. We have attempted to advocate throughout the book that student achievement should be used in conjunction with other evidence of teacher performance and productivity, and never in isolation. The challenge for educators and policy makers is to make certain that student achievement is placed in the broader context of multiple indicators of what teachers are accomplishing. Nonetheless, we think the conclusion is self-evident: teacher performance directly impacts student learning and, therefore, measures of student learning should be included in the process of assessing teacher quality. We believe that the four models presented in this book provide a range of possibilities for making this relationship more explicit and pronounced in the evaluation process. Assessing teacher quality is essential to fundamental education reform.

# Appendix A

## Qualities of Effective Teachers

## Prerequisites of Effective Teaching

| | |
|---|---|
| **Does intelligence relate to effective teaching?** | • Studies on this topic are limited and have had mixed results.<br>• Teacher verbal ability has been linked to student performance,[1] which may be a result of the connection between teachers' verbal abilities and their abilities to convey ideas in a clear and compelling way.[2] |
| **What is the relationship between teacher preparation and effective teaching?** | • Formal teacher preparation has a positive impact on student achievement in mathematics, science, and reading.[3]<br>• Content knowledge is important to effective teaching *up to a point.* The ability to present content to students in a meaningful way that fosters understanding is more important and not necessarily related to additional knowledge or coursework in the content area.[4]<br>• Teachers with formal training in meeting the needs of special populations of students (e.g., ESL, gifted and talented) are more effective with promoting achievement within these populations.[5] |

*Source:* Adapted with permission from James H. Stronge, *Qualities of Effective Teachers* (2002). Copyright © 2002 ASCD.

| **What is the relationship between certification status and effective teaching?** | • Teachers with certification of some kind (standard, alternative, or provisional) tend to have students with higher achievement rates than teachers working without certification.[6]<br>• Secondary teachers certified within their field have significantly higher student achievement rates than teachers working out-of-field.[7] |
| --- | --- |
| **What is the relationship between teaching experience and effectiveness?** | • Teachers with more experience tend to show better planning skills and greater differentiation of teaching strategies and learning activities. They also understand their students' learning needs better.[8]<br>• Teachers with more than three years of experience are more effective than those with less than three years; *however,* the benefits level off after about 5–8 years.[9] |

## The Teacher as a Person

| **What are the personality traits of an effective teacher?** | • Numerous studies have demonstrated the importance of caring in the eyes of teachers and students.<br>• Supervisors place priority on how teachers show students they are caring and supportive.<br>• Specific characteristics that are important include: listening, gentleness, understanding, warmth and encouragement, love for children.[10] |
| --- | --- |
| **According to students, what is the function of fairness and respect in effective teaching?** | • Important at all levels of schooling, from elementary through high school.<br><br>• *Effective teachers*<br>  – Respond to misbehavior at an individual level rather than hold a whole class responsible for the actions of a few;[11]<br>  – Demonstrate cultural respect, understanding, racial and cultural impartiality; and<br>  – Offer all students opportunities to participate and to succeed.[12] |

| How do effective teachers interact with their students? | • *Effective teachers*<br>  – Are perceived to be accessible and professional by students,<br>  – Are friendly and personable while maintaining appropriate teacher-student role structure,<br>  – Give students responsibility and respect,<br>  – Demonstrate interest in students' lives beyond the classroom,[13] and<br>  – Demonstrate a sense of fun and willingness to play.[14] |
| --- | --- |
| What is the effective teacher's attitude toward the profession of teaching? | • *Effective teachers*<br>  – Accept responsibility for student outcomes,[15]<br>  – Participate in a collegial, collaborative work environment,<br>  – Are involved in graduate study,[16] and<br>  – Hold high expectations of themselves as well as their students, and maintain a strong positive belief in their own efficacy.[17] |
| What is the role of reflective practice in effective teaching? | • Effective teachers dedicate extra hours to reflect on instruction and preparation.[18]<br>• Individually and collectively, there is a pattern of reflective practice among teachers in effective schools.[19] |

## Classroom Management and Organization

| What are the key classroom management skills of effective teachers? | • *Effective teachers*<br>  – Communicate clear rules and expectations for behavior from the very beginning of the school year,[20]<br>  – Establish procedures for routine, daily tasks, and needs,[21]<br>  – Maintain momentum via smooth transition of activities,[22]<br>  – Are able to engage in more than one action at the same time,<br>  – Move throughout the classroom to encourage attention, and<br>  – Anticipate potential problems and resolve minor distractions before they become major disruptions.[23] |
| --- | --- |

| How do effective teachers organize their classrooms? | • *Effective teachers*<br>– Have materials prepared in advance of the lesson, including extra materials;[24]<br>– Reinforce procedures that support students' knowledge of what to do and when, with a minimum of repetition of directions;[25] and<br>– Arrange learning space to efficiently store materials.[26] |
|---|---|

## Organizing and Orienting for Instruction

| How do effective teachers make the best use of instructional time? | • They prioritize instruction and student learning as the central purposes of schooling.[27]<br>• They maximize their allocated instructional time through effective classroom management and organizational skills in order to ensure smooth transitions, maintain momentum in the lesson, and limit disruptions.[28] |
|---|---|
| How do effective teachers plan for instruction? | • They identify clear lesson and learning objectives, and carefully link activities to them.<br>• They consider the following: organizing content presentation, selecting curriculum resources that reflect the objectives and student characteristics, incorporating graphic organizers, and preparing questions in advance to check for understanding and extend the learning opportunities.[29] |

## Implementing Instruction

| How do effective teachers enhance instruction? | • *Effective teachers*<br>– Use direct instruction, mastery learning, and guided and independent practice appropriately;[30]<br>– Apply hands-on learning;[31] and<br>– Solve problems across the curriculum by drawing on students' experiences.[32] |
|---|---|
| How do effective teachers communicate content and expectations to students? | • Clarity in the explanation of content is critical.[33]<br>• Dialogue is established about the understanding of the content through teacher and student questions.[34]<br>• When constructive feedback is provided, graded homework can have a positive effect on student achievement and communicates teachers' intentions.[35] |

| What is the relationship between student engagement in learning and effective teachers? | • To support increased student engagement, effective teachers vary instructional strategies, the types of activities, and assignments given.[36]<br>• Student engagement is maximized when students are involved in authentic activities related to the content under study.[37]<br>• Successful student engagement encourages a more positive attitude toward school.[38]<br>• Step-by-step directions, clear examples, and guided practice in an activity also contribute to high levels of student engagement and student success.[39] |

## Monitoring Student Progress and Potential

| How do effective teachers monitor student learning and utilize their findings to foster progress? | • *Effective teachers*<br>— Use pre-assessments to support targeted teaching of skills;<br>— Identify potential misconceptions that may occur during instruction and monitor students for signs of these misconceptions;[40]<br>— Reteach material to students who did not achieve mastery, and offer tutoring for students who seek additional help;<br>— Demonstrate effectiveness with the full range of student abilities in their classrooms, regardless of how academically diverse the students are;[41] and<br>— Provide timely and specific feedback to students.[42] |

# Appendix B

Testing and Assessment Methods

## Norm-Referenced Tests

| GENERAL | |
|---|---|
| **Assessment** | **Characteristics** |
| **Stanford Achievement Test (SAT9)** | K–12, norm-referenced, multiple choice (reading, mathematics, language, spelling, study skills, and listening) and open-ended subtests (reading, mathematics, science, social science, and language) |
| **Metropolitan Achievement Tests (MAT8)** | K–12, norm-referenced, multiple choice tests in reading, mathematics, language, science, and social studies |
| **Iowa Tests of Basic Skills (ITBS)** | K–12, norm-referenced, multiple choice tests, three versions of test with varying number of subtests |

| GENERAL | |
|---|---|
| **Assessment** | **Characteristics** |
| **California Achievement Tests (CAT/5)** | K–12, norm-referenced and curriculum-referenced, multiple choice tests, measures basic skills of reading, language, spelling, mathematics, study skills, science, and social studies; performance assessment component measures skills across several content areas |
| **Comprehensive Tests of Basic Skills (CTBS), 4th ed.** | K–12, norm-referenced and curriculum-referenced, multiple choice tests, measures basic skills of reading, language, spelling, mathematics, study skills, science, and social studies |
| **Riverside Curriculum Assessment System** | K–2, collection of test items and performance test that can be customized to an individual school district's curriculum objectives in reading/language arts, mathematics, social studies, and science |
| WRITING | |
| **Assessment** | **Characteristics** |
| **Writing Process Test** | 2–12, pre- and post-test versions |
| **CTB Writing Assessment System** | 2–12, independent or reading-related prompts |
| READING | |
| **Assessment** | **Characteristics** |
| **Test of Reading Comprehension (TORC-3)** | 2–12, measures silent reading comprehension, diagnostic |
| **Gates-MacGinitie Reading Tests, 3rd ed.** | K–12, measures vocabulary and comprehension |

| READING | |
| --- | --- |
| **Assessment** | **Characteristics** |
| **Stanford Diagnostic Reading Test (SDRT4)** | 1–12, diagnostic, measures decoding, vocabulary, comprehension, and scanning |
| **Gray Oral Reading Tests, 4th ed.** | K–12, measures oral reading rate and accuracy, oral reading comprehension, total oral reading ability, and oral reading miscues |
| **Degrees of Reading Power-Revised (DRP-R)** | 2–8, norm- and criterion-referenced, measures reading comprehension, three levels available |
| **Macmillan Individual Reading Analysis** | K–4, individually administered oral reading test |

## Criterion-Referenced Measures

| GENERAL | |
| --- | --- |
| **Assessment** | **Characteristics** |
| **Edutest** | Internet-based assessment and practice material for grades 2–8 in English, math, science, U.S. history, algebra 1 and 2, and geometry; replicates state assessments from California, Florida, Ohio, and Virginia |
| **Anecdotal Records Aligned with State Standards** | Informal tracking system, scored with a rubric |
| READING | |
| **Assessment** | **Characteristics** |
| **Phonemic Awareness Literacy Screening (PALS)** | K–3, measures knowledge of alphabetic code, screening |
| **Kindergarten Skills Assessment** | K, measures letter recognition, auditory discrimination, letter-sound relationships, classification, and sequencing |

| READING | |
| --- | --- |
| **Assessment** | **Characteristics** |
| **Standardized Reading Inventory (SRI), 2nd ed.** | 1–6, informal inventory of reading skills |
| **Monroe Standardized Silent Reading Tests** | 3–12, measures reading rate and comprehension |
| **Developmental Reading Assessment (DRA)** | K–3, individual test of oral reading development |
| **Flynt-Cooter Reading Inventory for the Classroom** | K–12, individual test of reading competencies, used to determine instructional level |
| **Accelerated Reader Program** | K–8, reading |
| **Qualitative Reading Inventory (QRI3)** | K–9, diagnostic purposes only |
| **Classroom Reading Inventory, 4th ed.** | 1–12, diagnostic purposes, global measure of instructional reading level |
| SPELLING | |
| **Assessment** | **Characteristics** |
| **Dolch Word List** | K–3, measures spelling and writing |
| **Developmental Spelling Analysis (DSA)** | Measures letter/name, within word, syllable juncture, and derivational consonant |
| **Buckingham Extension of Ayres Spelling Scale** | Spelling word bank for teachers to construct graded spelling lists |
| **Spelling Diagnostic Probe** | Spelling word bank organized by graded levels |

| WRITING | |
|---|---|
| **Assessment** | **Characteristics** |
| **ERB Writing Assessment Program** | 4–12, scored by two readers using 6-point scale |
| **State Benchmark Assessments** | Performance assessment based on established benchmarks or passing scores<br>Examples include<br>• Regent Exams in New York<br>• Assessment Program in Maryland (MSPAP)<br>• Tennessee Comprehensive Assessment Program (TCAP)<br>• Standards of Learning Tests in Virginia (SOL)<br>• Texas Assessment of Knowledge and Skills (TAKS) |

## Other Types of Student Assessments

| Authentic Assessment | Characteristics |
|---|---|
| **Writing Assessment** | Response to writing prompts that are scored using a rubric (such as n.s.–4) |
| **Portfolio** | Collection of artifacts and running records of performance that can be used for reading, math skills, and writing skills |
| **Exhibitions** | Work products that are judged by a teacher or panel of experts |
| **Performances** | Demonstrations of knowledge and/or skill in a "natural" manner |
| **Curriculum-Based Measurement/ Assessment** | Assessment of learning that (1) is "self-referenced," (2) provides comparison of individual student performance against self, and (3) answers the question of "How has the student improved over time in an area of study?" |

| Locally Developed Assessments | Characteristics |
|---|---|
| **Teacher-Made Tests** | Teacher-developed tests that are scored based on number correct or normal curve |
| **Departmental Tests** | Tests developed by a group of teachers to be used throughout the department to standardize curriculum goals |
| **Districtwide Tests** | Tests developed by a group of teachers with the support of curriculum specialists to measure course- or grade-level content in a more consistent manner |

# Appendix C

## Oregon Work Sample Methodology

*Directions:* Standards-based curriculum design can be a very complex and time-consuming task. To help you with this process, we have provided a structure for designing work samples. We have included a structure for the finished product and a "mental model" of the thinking process involved in creating the work sample.

**The finished components of the work sample (or unit of instruction) include:**

a. The unit topic.
b. The initial brainstormed graphic organizer.
c. The context and setting description.
d. Related national, state, and district goals.
e. Rationale for your unit.
f. Unit goals (largely derived from state and district curriculum goals).
g. The working graphic organizer.
h. The list of objectives to be taught to meet unit goals. Your goals and objectives need to be developed and aligned in the following format:

1.0  (list your first goal here)
1.1  (list the first lesson objective that matches your unit goal)
1.2  (list the second)
1.3  (and so on, until all of the objectives for this goal are listed)
2.0  (list your second goal here)
2.1  (list the first lesson objective that matches your unit goal)
2.2  (list the second)
2.3  (and so on, until all of the objectives for this goal are listed)
3.0  (list your third . . . final goal in a similar manner)
3.1  (list the first lesson objective that matches your unit goal)
3.2  (list the second)
3.3  (and so on until all of the objectives for this goal are listed)

i.  Lesson plans: Your work sample should contain well-developed lesson plans along with any supporting materials, transparencies, worksheets, manipulatives, or other resources that you might be using. Additionally, integrate with other content and literacy components, along with any expected special-needs modifications or extensions of the curriculum.

j.  Unit pre- and postassessment items for each unit goal and specific learning objectives.

k.  Pre-test and postassessment results displayed for each student and by cluster, with averages, a summary data table, and a chart of the summary results.

l.  Narrative data interpretation.

m. Reflective essay.

n.  Appendixes.

## The Initial Planning Process

In order to construct your brainstormed topic maps you'll need to engage in the following steps:

**1. Identify a unit topic:** Consider the content that you will be teaching. Determine what the class should be studying and what materials are available or needed. Next, come up with a unit topic.

**2. Brainstorm graphic organizer:** After selecting the topic, brainstorm subtopics for your unit. The final product of that brainstorming is a mind-map or graphic organizer that shows the major topic and related subtopics, along with important integrative connections.

**3. Identify context and setting:** Know your students: What are their needs and interests of your students? Next, analyze the setting in which you will teach the unit, including information related to

> a. The general socioeconomic level of the community in which your school exists (e.g., the percentage of students receiving free and reduced lunch).
>
> b. The prevailing cultural values reflected in the school setting (e.g., is there a daily newspaper?, what type of housing is available?).
>
> c. A thorough description of the school site (e.g., preschool, elementary, middle or high school, number of students, general school procedures, how problems are dealt with, composition of student makeup).
>
> d. A thorough description of the specific classroom (e.g., number of students, number of male and female students, cultural and linguistic makeup of students, number of special-needs students and their disabilities, number of ESL students, behavioral problems that you notice). What is the climate of the room like? Also include a section that describes the physical setup of the classroom, along with other information that you feel is pertinent, such as available technologies.

The above information will help you construct a work sample designed to accommodate the cultural, linguistic, and learning strengths and academic levels of the children in your classroom.

## Construct the Work Sample

**1. Brainstorm an initial graphic organizer.** Create your brainstormed graphic organizer. (If you're not a visual person and want to use a traditional outline, don't hesitate.) This will allow you to begin thinking about how your unit might be formed, and provide a way to facilitate discussion of your ideas.

**2. Use national, state, and district goals.** To enable your students to perform successfully on a required high-stakes assessment, you must align your topic with the local district, state, and national curriculum goals. Examine the district, state, and national goals in your content.

**3. Develop a rationale.** Think about why students should learn this topic. Why is it motivating or important? How does the unit fit with the existing curricular sequence or align with state standards? A rationale will help you plan your unit goals.

**4. Develop long-range goals for unit.** Design unit goals from both student interest and from the larger, curriculum goals that fit the cultural, linguistic, academic, and developmental needs of your students. These goals will vary in kind and complexity.

Examples:

- Related curriculum goal: *Students will recognize and explain relationships among events, issues, and developments in different spheres of human activity.*
- Your unit goal: *Students will examine, analyze, and identify common characteristics of various historical military leaders.*

**5. Create a working graphic organizer.** Revise your brainstormed graphic organizer to be a working graphic organizer. The goals, objectives, and lesson plans of your work sample will be generated from this initial planning, along with the lesson sequence, prerequisite tasks, integration with other content, and extensions or modifications for special-needs students.

**6. Specify performance outcomes and objectives for unit.** To ensure that students can meet unit goals, each goal should include two or three specific performance outcomes or objectives that are related to the lessons and the unit goals. These lesson objectives will be the backbone of your unit.

Example:

- Your unit goal: *Students will examine, analyze, and identify common characteristics of various historical military leaders.*

**7. Develop and align assessment items for each goal.** Design the pre- and postassessments for each unit goal and specific objectives. Although your pre- and postassessments need not be identical, they should be designed in order to be similar enough to reflect whether students actually mastered each of the objectives taught. Be sure to vary the levels of complexity and kinds of goals that you expect from your students, and consider alternative assessments for special-needs students.

**8. Pre-assess learners.** Determine what EACH student knows about EACH objective before you complete the final design of your unit lessons. Explain to your students that the pre-assessment is not graded, but will help you to deliver instruction best-suited to their needs and backgrounds.

**9. Analyze and record pre-assessment cluster data.** Analyze what EACH student knows and can demonstrate on EACH unit objective. In descending order, sort the scores for your students and divide the students into four clusters, of at least two students each, based on logical numeric groupings in your data. Not only will this information provide evidence of learning gains at the end, it also will help you design the unit itself and make decisions on individualizing instruction.

**10. Design lessons to meet student needs and align with unit goals.** In this section, you should include all of the lesson plans that you have developed for the unit. Although there are many ways to organize lesson plans, try to be consistent with a format that retains certain elements in common.

**11. Teaching and learning.** Teach your work sample and modify as needed to maximize daily and unit learning. Here are some suggestions:

    a. Incorporate various instructional and assessment strategies throughout your unit. Assess progress toward unit goals frequently, modifying your instruction accordingly.

    b. Attempt to justify the strategies that you choose. In other words, be able to defend how the strategy you chose will contribute to enhanced student learning of unit goals.

    c. Address the issue of differentiating your instruction for students with varied linguistic, cultural, academic, and developmental strengths. Also take into consideration different learning styles of your students.

**12. Postassess learners for each of your unit objectives.** Analyze data by student cluster, including calculating learning gains and cluster averages.

**13. Display your data.** Use a data table with pre- and postassessment data and learning gains calculations, displayed by cluster, then summarize the cluster averages, and chart (graph) your results for the clusters in order to compare learning gains by cluster. It might also be useful to chart the learning gains for each individual student, although visual inspection of the data table can provide that information just as well.

**14. Provide narrative interpretation of data.** Look at your results by cluster and, in a narrative format, interpret what learning gains you see (or do not see) and explain why they did or did not occur. Within each cluster, select individual students, where appropriate, whose results require specific comment.

**15. Reflection.** Consider the work sample. What did you learn while teaching? What seemed to work best in goal- or standards-based teaching for you? What would you change? How did your assessments work? How about differentiation of instruction for linguistic, cultural, academic, and developmental differences?

**16. Appendixes.** This section should include copies of all of the handouts, transparencies, reading lists, materials lists, and other materials you have generated as resources for helping teach the lessons. The goal is to display a representative sampling of the variety of student work.

*Source:* The process for developing a comprehensive instructional unit depicted in this appendix is adapted from the Western Oregon University strategy used with student teachers. Some of the elements in the lesson unit design may be adapted, whereas others may be considered unnecessary. Reprinted with permission.

# Appendix D

## Thompson (Colorado) School District
## Teacher Standards, Tools, and Strategies

*Source:* Reprinted with permission of the Thompson School District.

| Pre-Observation Tool | Instruction | Standards 1–4 |
|---|---|---|

School Professional:_____ Position:_____

Please meet with me on_____ (Time)_____ for a Pre-Observation Conference.

Postobservation Conference Date &Time: _____

### STANDARDS-BASED PLANNING

*Please be prepared for this conference by having the following information ready.*

1. List the subject area of the observation and standard or benchmark that will be addressed.

2. Describe the concept of the lesson (e.g., subtraction).

3. Please suggest a time you would like for a formal observation:

   Date: _____ Time: _____ Location: _____

4. Pre-assessment analysis or a description of how you will pre-assess. Please describe the assessment or bring it with you.

5. What will you use for a postassessment? Please bring it with you, including the scoring guide or rubric.

6. Please bring any other important information that needs to be shared.

| Pre-Observation Tool | Instruction | Standards 1–5 |

School Professional: _____ Date: _____ Pre-Observation: _____

Observation Date & Time: _____ Postobservation Date & Time: _____

Observation Setting: _____

## DATA-DRIVEN INSTRUCTION PLANNING

*This can be a self-evaluation tool for new teachers or teachers in a new role. It can be used to help a teacher prepare for an observation and conference. It is also a pre-observation tool based on standards and data-driven instruction. Where possible, the school professional should cite specific examples and evidence. This tool could also be used for data collection during an observation by the evaluator.*

**Arrange for your observation time and pre-observation conference. Then, please take the time to fill in the following information and return it to your evaluator at least one day prior to the observation. Thank you!**

1. Identify the standard or standards and benchmarks addressed in this lesson. How will you communicate these to students?

2. What pre-assessment did you use to base your decision on, to teach this lesson? Elaborate on the assessment analysis and scoring criteria. Please attach.

3. What must students know and be able to remember years from now as a result of this instruction?

4. How will students know that they have done well on this lesson? Please attach your scoring criteria for this lesson or the rubric for the unit.

5. What models will you use to demonstrate proficient and advanced levels of performance on this lesson? Please attach or describe models.

6. What instructional strategies and resources will you use to help students perform well on the assessment? Relate your choice to the pre-assessment results or to the desired performance on the final assessment for the unit.

7. What modifications have you preplanned for learners who are below proficiency and for those at the advanced level? Please attach any examples.

8. Attach the final assessment including the scoring guide or rubric.

*Adapted from Lamar RE-2 School District Pre-Observation Tools, designed by Terri Quackenbush, 1999.*

**Pre-Observation Tool**            Instruction            Standards 1–5

School Professional:_____ Position:_____

Date of Pre-Observation Conference: _____

Date of Observation:_____ Time: _____ Setting/Activity: _____

## STANDARDS-BASED CLASSROOMS

*This can be used as a pre-observation tool for note taking during the conference, or to have the teacher fill out prior to observation. Administrators can also use this guide to note evidence of data-driven instruction.*

1.  What will you be teaching? (Standard)

2.  On what basis have you decided to teach this lesson? (Pre-assessment)

3.  What will your students know and be able to do as a result of your instruction (e.g., benchmark, indicator, skills)?

4.  How will you know they have demonstrated this thinking, skill, knowledge, or product? (Indicate type of evaluation)

5.  What criteria will you use? (Indicate design of assessment)

6.  What special learning needs and styles must you account for in your instruction? (Unique learners)

7.  What instructional strategies will you use? Why?

8.  What materials must you prepare?

9.  How will the learning environment look?

10. Given the questions above, what aspect of data-driven instruction is your primary focus for this lesson?

Self-Evaluation Tool                Instruction                Standards 1–5

School Professional: _____ Date: _____ Setting: _____

Other Comments:_____

## USING NEW INSTRUCTIONAL STRATEGIES

*This self-evaluation tool may be useful to new teachers, or teachers in a new role, as a postob-servation tool. It may also make a good tool to use as an indicator for one's professional goals. Administrators may use it for reflection in postobservation or goal development conferences.*

**Trying different instructional strategies helps to differentiate instruction for learners with all types of needs. Some instructional strategies may result in greater achievement by students or promote a classroom atmosphere that encourages good discipline and student well-being.**

1. An instructional strategy I have chosen:

2. Description of how I will use this strategy:

3. My reason for wanting to extend the use of this strategy or to learn how to use it:

4. The way I will assess the success of this strategy in meeting the needs of unique learners:

*Adapted from Portfolio Assessment: Teacher Self-Evaluation.*

Pre- or Postobservation Tool          Instruction              Standards 1–5

School Professional:_____ Position:_____

Date of Pre-Observation: _____ Date & Time of Postobservation Conference: _____

Date of Observation:_____ Time: _____ Setting/Activity: _____

## PRE- AND POSTOBSERVATION:
## USING A VARIETY OF INSTRUCTIONAL STRATEGIES

1. *This tool can be used as a self-evaluation tool for school professionals.*
2. *It can also be used as a pre- or postobservation tool.*
3. *It may also make a good tool to use as an indicator for professional growth goals.*
4. *Administrators may use these prompts for reflection in postobservation or goal development conferences.*

Varying your instructional strategies helps to differentiate instruction for learners with all types of needs. Some instructional strategies may result in greater achievement by students while promoting a classroom atmosphere that encourages good discipline and student well-being.

### Before the Observation:

1. An instructional strategy that I think increases the probability of student achievement is:

2. Description of the instruction technique or strategy:

3. My analysis of prior student performance led me to choose this strategy because:

4. The way I will assess the success of this strategy:

### After the Observation:

1. How did this strategy work?

2. How do you know? (Provide assessment results)

3. Will you use it again? Why or why not?

4. Under what circumstances might you use it again? How could you make it better?

Pre-Observation Tool                Instruction                Standards 1–4

School Professional: _____ Pre-Observation Date: _____

Observation Setting:_____ Date & Time:_____

Postobservation Date &Time: _____

### PLANNING FOR ASSESSMENT

*Complete 1, 2, 3, and 4 and submit this form to your evaluator at least one day prior to your observation. You will need to complete question 5 prior to your postobservation conference.*

1. List the targeted content standard and benchmarks:


2. What observable student actions will demonstrate proficient learning?


3. Design an assessment that will measure the students' learning as it relates to the benchmark for this lesson. Please attach it, along with any models you have of proficient or higher work. Decide what specific skills are a prerequisite to successfully perform on the assessment. Please list the skills below:


4. What instructional strategies for this lesson will engage students and prepare them for the assessment?


5. Analyze the assessment results from this lesson to determine how students performed.


*Adapted for Thompson School District, Loveland, Colorado.*

| Data Collection Tool | Instruction | Standard 3 |
|---|---|---|

School Professional: _____ Date: _____ Setting: _____

Other Comments:_____

## USING EXPECTATIONS AND ASSESSMENTS IN INSTRUCTION

*This instrument can be used to evaluate the quality of a school professional's classroom assessment process. Evaluators can use specific examples of tests, analysis of assessment, or they can observe the results of the assessment of data in the form of lesson plans based on those data.*

Mark an "X" in front of the statements that are applicable.

**Comments**

**Test content**

_____Assessment includes higher-level thinking skills

**Presentation of test to students**

_____Assessment presented to students to highlight critical learning and purpose of assessment

**Communication of expectations to students**

_____Communicates the ethics and skills of test-taking

**Results reviewed with class**

_____Assessment results reviewed and discussed with class or student

**Assessment follow-up**

_____Teacher arranges for remediation with those who do not meet minimal standards and retests to see that they reach those standards

_____Teacher arranges for enrichment or alternative instruction for those who already meet standards on a pre-assessment

**Student self-assessment**

_____Teacher utilizes assessment to assist students in self-evaluation of performance

**Use of assessment**

_____Teacher uses assessment analysis to plan future instruction and determine student performance levels

_____Data analysis is used to determine the effectiveness of instruction

**Postobservation Tool**　　　　　Instruction　　　　　Standards 1–5

School Professional: _____ Pre-Observation Date and Time:_____

Observation Date & Time:_____ Setting: _____

Postobservation Date & Time: _____

## REFLECTION: ASSESSMENT PLAN

*This tool can be used as a postobservation form to be filled out by the teacher or to guide a postobservation conference.*

List the instructional standards and benchmarks: _____

_____

Specify types of assessments used: _____

_____

1. What are the distinctive features of this assessment that caused you to select it?

2. On what assessment data did you base your selection of strategies?

3. What common or uncommon variations on this assessment did you put into place for this lesson or unit?

4. What is the primary purpose or instructional information that this type of assessment gives to you?

5. What did you see as the advantages of this assessment?

6. What did you see as the disadvantages of this assessment?

7. On what kind of data analysis did you base your evaluation of the success of this assessment?

8. If you used this assessment again, would you change anything? Why?

*Taken in part from Peter Airasian and Arlen Gullickson, Teacher Self-Evaluation Tool Kit, Corwin Press, Inc., Thousand Oaks, CA, 1997.*

School Professional Evaluation Tool    Professional Growth    Standards 7–10

School Professional: _____ Date: _____ Setting: _____

Other Comments:_____

## PROFESSIONAL GROWTH PLANS

*School professionals can use this self-evaluation tool for monitoring the progress of their professional goals. Administrators may use it for (1) reflection questions, (2) general data collection, or (3) goal development conferences. Evidence, observations, or examples can be cited and indicators checked. The school professional uses a written professional development plan as a guide to self-improvement and learning, and then analyzes the results of that plan.*

### Part One: Creating a Professional Growth Plan
_____a.  The plan has defined professional growth, instructional growth, and improvement goals, and has activities designed to accomplish those goals.
_____b.  The plan has been developed through a collaborative process between the school professional and the administrator based on self-assessments and data.
_____c.  The plan supports school or district instructional priorities.
_____d.  The school professional assumes responsibility for managing the agreed-on plan and sees that activities are completed in a timely manner.
_____e.  The school professional and the administrator review the plan periodically. The plan is modified when appropriate.

### Part Two: Implementing the Growth Plan
_____a.  The school professional is able to identify specific professional and instructional improvements that have taken place as a result of the growth plan.
_____b.  The school professional reads professional books and articles related to the growth plan and to the assignment.
_____c.  The school professional attends workshops, graduate school classes, and conferences related to the growth plan.
_____d.  The school professional serves on school- or district-level committees.

### Part Three: Analyzing the Results of the Professional Growth Plan
_____a.  The school professional demonstrates the accomplishment of each indicator on the goal plan by creating a written summary with analysis and attaching examples or artifacts.
_____b.  The written analysis describes the impact of the professional growth activities.
_____c.  The analysis and artifacts are presented in an edited, typewritten, and professional manner.
_____d.  The school professional analyzes the success of the plan and indications for further growth or implementation.

### Other notable activities and progress:

# Appendix E

### Resources, Definitions, and Performance Responsibilities

## Contributing Public School Divisions

*Virginia:*
Charles City County Public Schools
Dinwiddie County Public Schools
Hampton City Public Schools
King and Queen County Public Schools
King William County Public Schools
Northumberland County Public Schools
Virginia Beach City Public Schools
Westmoreland County Public Schools
Williamsburg-James City County Public Schools

*Michigan:*
Lenawee Intermediate School District

# Definitions: Teacher Performance Domains

| Domain | Definition |
|--------|-----------|
| **Instruction** | This domain encompasses both organizing for instruction and delivery of instruction. The major responsibilities include planning and implementing a variety of activities consistent with instructional objectives, and selecting instructional methods compatible with student abilities and learning styles. The goal of all instruction is to create learning experiences that result in measurable student achievement. |
| **Assessment** | This domain includes the processes of gathering, reporting, and using a variety of data in a consistent manner to measure achievement, plan instruction, and improve student performance. |
| **Learning Environment** | This domain reflects the creation of a positive learning environment by using resources, routines, and procedures that provide a productive, safe classroom that promotes student learning. |
| **Communications & Community Relations** | This domain describes the responsibilities of teachers to use effective communication strategies in working with students, parents, and members of the community to promote support for student learning. |
| **Professionalism** | This domain defines the standards for demonstrating a commitment to professional ethics and growth, while advancing the mission of the school division. |

*Source:* Reprinted with permission of Alexandria City Public Schools.

# Teacher Performance Responsibilities

| Domain | Performance Responsibility |
|---|---|
| **Instruction** | I-1: The teacher demonstrates current and accurate knowledge of subject matter covered in the curriculum.<br>I-2: The teacher plans instruction to achieve desired student learning objectives that reflect current division and state curriculum standards.<br>I-3: The teacher uses materials and resources that are comparable with students' needs and abilities, and that support the approved curriculum.<br>I-4: The teacher differentiates instruction to meet diverse student needs.<br>I-5: The teacher promotes student learning through the effective use of instructional strategies. |
| **Assessment** | A-1: The teacher uses a variety of ongoing and culminating assessments to measure student progress.<br>A-2: The teacher uses student performance data in instructional planning and decision making.<br>A-3: The teacher provides ongoing and timely feedback to encourage student progress. |
| **Learning Environment** | E-1: The teacher maximizes the use of instructional time to increase student learning.<br>E-2: The teacher organizes the classroom to ensure an environment that is safe and conducive to student learning.<br>E-3: The teacher manages appropriate student behavior. |
| **Communications & Community Relations** | C-1: The teacher communicates effectively and appropriately with students.<br>C-2: The teacher maintains timely communication with parent or guardians concerning student progress or problems.<br>C-3: The teacher communicates and collaborates effectively with the school and school community. |
| **Professionalism** | P-1: The teacher demonstrates moral and ethical behavior appropriate to the profession.<br>P-2: The teacher participates in an ongoing process of professional development.<br>P-3: The teacher contributes to the profession, the school, the school division, and the community. |

*Source:* Reprinted with permission of Alexandria City Public Schools.

# Appendix F

## Tennessee Framework, Rubrics, and Forms for Evaluation

### Framework for Evaluation and Professional Growth

The current Tennessee State Model for Local Evaluation was adopted in 1988. The foundation of this model is a set of competencies and indicators presented as minimum standards and based on teacher effectiveness research. Traditional evaluation procedures include pre-observations, completion of approved evaluation documents, and postobservation conferences.

#### Documenting the Need for Change

In 1995, the State Board of Education Master Plan included the need to re-evaluate the State Model for Local Evaluation based on current initiatives within Tennessee, as well as the introduction of the National Standards for Beginning Teachers. Revisions to the local evaluation process were to reflect the acceptance and encouragement of multiple teaching methods, attention to national standards, and the use of student performance information.

*Source:* Reprinted with permission of the Tennessee Department of Education.

Considered in the development of the Framework for Evaluation and Professional Growth were *The Tennessee School Improvement Planning Process: A Blueprint for Continuous Learning* (1996); proposed revisions to the *Tennessee Licensure Standards: Professional Education* (1997), *Model Standards for Beginning Teacher Licensing: A Resource for State Dialogue* by the Interstate New Teacher Assessment and Support Consortium (1992); *Tennessee School-to-Career System, Executive Summary* (1996); and emerging research regarding clinical supervision and developmental supervision. Evaluation models in other states, as well as Canada, were reviewed.

Given the above, the Framework for Evaluation and Professional Growth was designed to facilitate the implementation of current initiatives within the state, such as the introduction of the Curriculum and Instruction Frameworks and the school improvement process, as well as improve the quality of the evaluation process for all teachers. An emphasis has been placed throughout the evaluation process on developing and assessing the capacity to improve student performance.

### Purpose

The purposes for which teacher evaluation will be used are as follows:

*1. Accountability:* to assure that evaluation considers effectiveness in the classroom and within the school.

*2. Professional Growth:* to provide a focus for professional growth in an area that has the greatest capacity for facilitating improved student performance.

*3. Cohesive School Structure:* to increase and focus the dialogue within schools on the goal of improved services to students.

The Framework for Evaluation and Professional Growth was designed to meet the above stated goals and provides for an evaluation process which requires the examination of:

- What students need to know and be able to do,
- What the teacher has been doing to affect this learning,
- The degree of student success in achieving those objectives, and
- The implications for continuing employment and future professional growth.

## Beliefs and Principles

•  Each teacher should possess a repertoire of teaching strategies. The content, purposes of instruction, and needs of students should drive the selection and implementation of appropriate strategies.

•  Effectiveness of teaching behavior must be assessed in light of student, school, and school system characteristics, needs, and organizational structures; student performance; and long-term as well as short-term instructional effectiveness.

•  Multiple sources of data are essential for the development of a complete picture of teaching performance.

•  The evaluation process must accommodate the needs of novice educators as well as the differing needs of experienced educators.

•  The evaluation process must be understood by all teachers and evaluators.

•  There must be a direct link between evaluation results and planned professional growth.

## Framework for Evaluation and Professional Growth: Components

In recognizing the differing needs of students, teachers, schools, and school systems, the framework contains two major evaluation components—*Comprehensive Assessment and Professional Growth* and *Focused Assessment and Professional Growth.*

The comprehensive assessment component is used to assess novice (apprentice) educators. This component is also suitable for experienced educators who request or require structured input from a supervisor or administrator. This model contains the necessary structure to provide a comprehensive picture of the educator's performance as well as a focus for future growth.

School systems and educators have the option of implementing the second component—Focused Assessment and Professional Growth. This component can only be used with professionally licensed personnel and begins with an identification of the current performance level based on previous evaluations, the educator's self-assessment, and student performance information. Given this information, a growth goal and Professional Growth Plan is designed by the educator with administrator input.

The growth plan must contain the following:

1. Areas to be strengthened (areas for growth) identified based on evidence of student performance collected through a variety of assessment techniques and attention to the performance standards;

2. Statement of the Professional Growth Goals and Objectives;

3. Outline of the action plan including a timeline for completion;

4. Identification of the evaluation methods and criteria that will be used to assess progress and growth as a result of the implementation of the plan; and

5. Statement of expected benefits with emphasis placed upon the impact of the educator's growth on student performance.

The growth plan is reviewed and approved for implementation based on the following criteria:

• Does the plan logically address an identified area to strengthen for the educator, grade level, school, and system?

• Does the plan provide evidence that the resulting educator growth has the capacity to improve student performance?

• Do the evaluation methods as identified in the plan provide appropriate monitoring of the growth process and the impact on student performance? Has the educator identified reasonable and specific indicators of student success?

According to the nature of the educator's professional growth goal, the action plan may provide for any combination of the following: classroom observations; research and study for the purpose of strengthening content and pedagogical or professional skills; action research; collaborations; and the use of a cognitive coach during the implementation phase with students.

The evaluator monitors the implementation of the plan and conducts a goal evaluation summative conference at the end of the evaluation period. The Focused Assessment Summative Report will be completed. *The evaluator retains the right to conduct classroom observations and review other data as needed.*

## Summary

The Framework for Evaluation and Professional Growth provides flexibility for both the school system and the educator. The Comprehensive Assessment and Professional Growth is the only required component of the framework. School systems may choose to implement the Focused Assessment and Professional Growth component in order to more effectively tailor the evaluation to align with identified student needs, educator needs, school improvement plans, and system needs, as well as build on the existing knowledge of an educator's performance.

## Comprehensive Assessment and Professional Growth: Teacher and Evaluator Activities

### Target Group

This is the required assessment component for apprentice teachers, and it may be required for all nontenured personnel, if the system desires. It is also suitable for experienced teachers who request or require structured input from an administrator. This model provides a comprehensive picture of the educator's performance and effectiveness with students, as well as a focus for future growth.

### Teacher Activities

- Use a variety of data sources to complete a *self-assessment*. Three areas of strength and three areas for growth are identified, based on *performance standards* and evidence of student performance collected through a variety of assessment techniques.

- Complete a *planning information record* for each announced and unannounced observation. This will include information about the teacher's decision-making process for this group of students, how student data was used to design this lesson, and what data will be gathered to identify this lesson's effectiveness.

- Complete a *reflecting information record* after each observation. Links will be established between effective teacher behaviors and the actual data gathered to assess student learning.

• Compile work samples in the *Educator Information Record* and submit prior to the last observation. This provides an opportunity to document non-observable behaviors in the areas of assessment and professional growth.

• Develop a *future growth plan* to be implemented after the evaluation process is complete. The depth of this plan may depend on the evaluation cycle and whether the plan is allowed to exist over more than one evaluation period.

## Evaluator Activities

• Review prior evaluations.

• Orient the teacher to the evaluation process and have input into the discussion of strengths, areas for growth, and identification of areas for refinement during the evaluation process.

• Probe any areas of the planning process (*planning information record*) for clarification or depth.

• Record notes regarding the events and facts of all classroom observations (at least three observations for a 1st and 2nd year apprentice—at least two observations for a 3rd year apprentice and someone professionally licensed).

• Look for evidence of the teacher as a reflective practitioner who can analyze student performance data in relation to his or her own classroom behaviors (*reflecting information record*).

• Provide feedback for the entire observation process (planning, observation, reflecting) on the *appraisal record.*

• Review the *Educator Information Record.*

• Complete the *Comprehensive Assessment—Summative Report.*

• Discuss the performance levels identified on the *Summative Report* and identify areas for the *Future Growth Plan.*

## COMPREHENSIVE ASSESSMENT
### *EDUCATOR INFORMATION RECORD*

EDUCATOR NAME: _____ SCHOOL NAME:_____

The purpose of this record is to gather a sampling of information regarding the Assessment and Evaluation and Professional Growth Domains. The evaluator may ask for further clarification of this information. You may record information on these pages or reproduce them exactly as they appear.

### Domain III: Assessment and Evaluation

1. For each category below, provide information regarding the most effective assessment you have used, an example of results obtained, and how this data was used to make instructional decisions.

**Pre-Assessment** *(How do you determine the students' entry level prior to instruction?)* **IIIA**

| Assessment Description (You may attach a copy of the assessment.) | What were the results? | How have you used the results? |
|---|---|---|
|  |  |  |

**Ongoing Progress** *(How do you determine the students' progress as a result of instruction?)* **IIIB**

| Assessment Description (You may attach a copy of the assessment.) | What were the results? | How have you used the results? |
|---|---|---|
|  |  |  |

**Assessment of Strategies and Techniques** *(How do you determine the effectiveness of your strategies and techniques with these students?)* **IIIC**

| Assessment Description (You may attach a copy of the assessment.) | What were the results? | How have you used the results? |
|---|---|---|
|  |  |  |

2. If you have received a Tennessee Value-Added Assessment System (TVAAS) Teacher Report with a 3-year average, please respond to the following:

a) After analyzing the TVAAS data, what have you learned about your techniques or strategies and the resulting student performance?

b) How have you used this data to make instructional decisions?

3.  Provide one example of pre- or postdata for a class of students. Describe the amount of student progress exhibited and how your conclusions were used to make instructional decisions. (You may attach copies of the assessments.) **IIID**

| Pre-Instruction Data | Postinstruction Data | Conclusions |
|---|---|---|
|  |  |  |

Use of this Information:

4.  What are two of your *most effective* methods for communicating with parents and appropriate others? (Describe and provide examples.) **IIIB**

### Domain V: Professional Growth

5. A collaboration is defined as an intellectual endeavor where two or more educators share with each other and gain from each other professional knowledge. It is understood that educators regularly engage in professional growth opportunities such as collaborative and professional development activities. Complete the following chart providing information regarding recent collaborative activities. **VA**

| Collaborative Activity and Date | Purpose of Collaboration | Outcome of the Collaboration |
|---|---|---|
|  |  |  |
|  |  |  |

6. Use the chart provided below to provide information regarding two of your most useful professional growth activities. Include a description of your application of these professional growth opportunities in your classroom as well as information regarding any professional leadership with colleagues that might have resulted from your growth. **VB**

| Professional Development Activity and Date | Application and Leadership that have Resulted from the Professional Development Activity |
|---|---|
|  |  |
|  |  |

# RUBRICS

PERFORMANCE STANDARDS
DOMAIN III:     ASSESSMENT AND EVALUATION
INDICATOR A.  Uses appropriate assessment strategies and instruments to obtain
                    information about students and their ongoing progress and uses this
                    information to make instructional decisions

## PERFORMANCE LEVEL A

Assessment is primarily used to document student performance. Grades and scores are based on assessment results with limited use of this assessment for diagnosis and instruction. Assessment is used to measure student learning at the end of units of study. General monitoring (i.e., questions, homework) is used to identify students' status. Reteaching is used when general class misunderstanding is demonstrated.

## PERFORMANCE LEVEL B

Assessment is used at the beginning of the year to make instructional decisions regarding the course of study. Appropriate assessment methods and instruments are selected for the outcomes being measured. Assessment strategies (formal or informal) are used to elicit information regarding student experiences, modes of learning, needs, attitudes and progress. All forms of assessment are appropriately administered and the results are accurately interpreted. This data is used when making instructional decisions throughout the year.

## PERFORMANCE LEVEL C

An understanding of measurement theory and assessment related issues (i.e., validity, reliability, bias, scoring concerns) is demonstrated through the use and interpretation of all types of assessment. Given this understanding, teacher-made tests show appropriate construction for measuring intended outcomes. Ongoing assessment is accurately and systematically used to plan, refine, and modify the students' instruction. Remediation, instruction, or enrichment is based on the diagnosis of the point of learning as opposed to a general understanding or misunderstanding. Appropriate techniques are used during instruction to assess student understanding and mastery of the goals and objectives.

*Data Sources:* Educator Information Record, Planning Information Records, Classroom Observations, Reflecting Information Records, Educator Conferences

# RUBRICS

PERFORMANCE STANDARDS
DOMAIN III:     ASSESSMENT AND EVALUATION
INDICATOR B.  Communicates student status and progress to students, their parents,
and appropriate others

## PERFORMANCE LEVEL A

Cumulative student reports are provided to students, parents, and appropriate others at required intervals. Students are provided general feedback reflecting the correctness or incorrectness of their responses. Required records of student work and performance are maintained.

## PERFORMANCE LEVEL B

Students are regularly informed of the accuracy of their responses and of their status regarding the accomplishment of goals and objectives. Additionally, parents and appropriate others are informed on a timely basis of a student's status, as well as academic and affective changes. Routines have been established for two-way communication with students, parents, and appropriate others.

## PERFORMANCE LEVEL C

Diagnostic and prescriptive information is provided to students, parents, and appropriate others for the purpose of improving performance. Attention is focused on what needs to be done to move to the next performance level. Communication strategies have been refined to ensure that parent and student feedback will affect a change. Useful records of student work and performance are maintained.

*Data Sources:* Educator Information Record, Classroom Observations, Educator Conferences

# RUBRICS

PERFORMANCE STANDARDS
DOMAIN III:     ASSESSMENT AND EVALUATION
INDICATOR C. Reflects on teaching practice by evaluating continually the effects of
                instruction

## PERFORMANCE LEVEL A

Assessment focuses on student achievement with limited connections made to the effectiveness of the strategies or techniques employed. The educator's reflections include an accurate description of classroom behaviors, including sequence of events, teacher and student behaviors, and time frames. Given this accurate description, the educator can determine an overall level of success.

## PERFORMANCE LEVEL B

A variety of assessment results are used to determine the relationship between student success and teacher behaviors. The educator can accurately interpret these results in terms of the effectiveness of the strategies or techniques employed. Modifications, adaptations, and refinements in teaching strategies and behaviors are made based on the accurate interpretation of this data.

## PERFORMANCE LEVEL C

The teacher can communicate specific examples of the cyclical process of reflection, assessment, and learning. Classroom data, information about student progress, and research are used as sources for evaluating the outcomes of teaching and learning and as a basis for experimenting with, reflecting on, and revising practice.

*Data Sources:* Educator Information Record, Reflecting Information Records, Educator Conferences

## RUBRICS

PERFORMANCE STANDARDS
DOMAIN III:     ASSESSMENT AND EVALUATION
INDICATOR D.  Evaluates student performance and determines the amount of
                    progress

### PERFORMANCE LEVEL A

Grades or cumulative scores are cited as evidence of student growth. The use of baseline
data is limited in the interpretation of student learning. General statements are provided
to document formal and informal assessment of both academic growth and positive attitu-
dinal change.

### PERFORMANCE LEVEL B

Assessment techniques are used to determine students' performance level prior to and
after instruction. The amount of student growth and possible intervening variables are
communicated knowledgeably. Assessment strategies may be limited in type but include
structured measurement of both cognitive and affective domains. The teacher can communicate the accuracy and usefulness of the data.

### PERFORMANCE LEVEL C

Appropriate assessment techniques are used to evaluate what students know and are
able to do as a result of instruction. Both cognitive and affective assessments are appropriately used to provide a more complete profile of student growth. Student growth is communicated knowledgeably and responsibly. Knowledge and understanding of any
intervening variables is used to determine an accurate amount of progress.

*Data Sources:* Educator Information Record, Reflecting Information Records, Educator Conferences

# Notes

## Chapter 1

1. See Darling-Hammond, L. (2000). Teacher quality and student achievement: A review of state policy evidence. *Education Policy Analysis Archives, 8*(1). Retrieved January 22, 2004 from http://olam.ed.asu.edu/epaa/v8n1/ and Stronge, J. H. (2002). *Qualities of effective teachers.* Alexandria, VA: Association for Supervision and Curriculum Development.
2. Marzano, R. J., Pickering, D. J., & Pollock, J. E. (2001). *Classroom instruction that works: Research-based strategies for increasing student achievement.* Alexandria, VA: Association for Supervision and Curriculum Development.
3. Schmoker, M. (1999). *Results: The key to continuous school improvement.* Alexandria, VA: Association for Supervision and Curriculum Development, p. 70.
4. The Tennessee Value-Added Research and Assessment Center work will be highlighted in more detail in Chapter 6.
5. Sanders, W. L., & Rivers, J. C. (1996). *Cumulative and residual effects of teachers on future student academic achievement* (Research Progress Report). Knoxville, TN: University of Tennessee Value-Added Research and Assessment Center.
6. Wright, S. P., Horn, S. P., & Sanders, W. L. (1997). Teacher and classroom context effects on student achievement: Implications for teacher evaluation. *Journal of Personnel Evaluation in Education, 11*, 57–67, p. 63.
7. Sanders & Rivers, 1996, p. 63.
8. Wright, Horn, & Sanders, 1997, p. 57.
9. Jordan, H., Mendro, R., & Weerasinghe, D. (1997, July). *Teacher effects on longitudinal student achievement.* Paper presented at the sixth National Evaluation Institute sponsored by CREATE, Indianapolis, IN.
10. Mendro, R. L. (1998). Student achievement and school and teacher accountability. *Journal of Personnel Evaluation in Education, 12*, 257–267, p. 262. The Dallas Public Schools program will be highlighted in more detail in Chapter 6.
11. Mendro, 1998, p. 261.
12. Mendro, 1998, p. 261.
13. Schmoker, 1999, p. 2.

14. Duke, D. L. (1990). Developing teacher evaluation systems that promote professional growth. *Journal of Personnel Evaluation in Education, 4*, 131–144; McLaughlin, M. W., & Pfeiffer, R. S. (1988). *Teacher evaluation: Improvement, accountability, and effective learning.* New York: Teachers College Press; Stronge, J. H. (1997). Improving schools through teacher evaluation. In J. H. Stronge (Ed.), *Evaluating teaching: A guide to current thinking and best practice* (pp. 1–23). Thousand Oaks, CA: Corwin Press.

15. Iwanicki, E. F. (1990). Teacher evaluation for school improvement. In J. Millman and L. Darling-Hammond (Eds.), *The new handbook of teacher evaluation: Assessing elementary and secondary school teachers* (pp. 158–171). Newbury Park, CA: Sage.

16. McGahie, W. C. (1991). Professional competence evaluation. *Educational Researcher, 20*, 3–9.

17. Educational Research Service. (1988). *Teacher evaluation: Practices and procedures.* Arlington, VA: Author.

18. Medley, D. M., Coker, H., & Soar, R. S. (1984). *Measurement-based evaluation of teacher performance.* New York: Longman.

19. Stronge, J. H., & Tucker, P. D. (2003). *Handbook on teacher evaluation: Assessing and improving performance.* Larchmont, NY: Eye on Education.

20. Schalock, H. D. (1998). Student progress in learning: Teacher responsibility, accountability and reality. *Journal of Personnel Evaluation in Education, 12*(3), 237–246.

21. Schalock, 1998, p. 237.

22. Howard, B. B., & McColskey, W. H. (2001). Evaluating experienced teachers. *Educational Leadership, 58*(5), 48–51, p. 49.

23. Cawelti, G. (1999). *Portraits of six benchmark schools: Diverse approaches to improving student achievement.* Arlington, VA: Educational Research Service; Schmoker, M. (2001). *The results handbook.* Alexandria, VA: Association for Supervision and Curriculum Development; Skrla, L., Scheurich, J. J., & Johnson, J. F. (2000). *Equity-driven achievement-focused school districts.* Austin, TX: Charles A. Dana Center.

24. Viadero, D. (2004, January 21). Achievement-gap study emphasizes better use of data. *Education Week,* p. 9.

25. Schmoker, 1999, p. 39.

26. Schmoker, 1999, p. 44.

27. Lortie, D. C. (1975). *School-teacher: A sociological study.* Chicago: University of Chicago Press, p.141.

28. National Commission on Teaching and America's Future. (1996). *What matters most: Teaching for America's future.* New York: Author.

29. National Commission on Teaching and America's Future, 1996, p. 18.

30. Although there are good examples of school-based performance assessment systems, we chose to exclude those from this study and, rather, to concentrate on approaches that focus on individual teacher performance and student learning.

## Chapter 2

1. McConney, A. A., Schalock, M. D., & Schalock, H. D. (1997). Indicators of student learning in teacher evaluation. In J. H. Stronge (Ed.), *Evaluating teaching: A guide to current thinking and best practice* (pp. 162–192). Thousand Oaks, CA: Corwin Press, p. 162.

2. Frymier, J. (1998). Accountability and student learning. *Journal of Personnel Evaluation in Education, 12*, 233–235.

3. Eisner, E. W. (1999). The uses and limits of performance assessment. *Phi Delta Kappan, 80*, 658–660.

4. National Commission on Teaching & America's Future. (1996). *What matters most: Teaching for America's future.* New York: Author, p. 3.

5. Brophy, J., & Good, T. (1986). Teacher behavior and student achievement. In M. C. Wittrock (Ed.), *Handbook of Research on Teaching* (pp. 328–375). New York: MacMillan.

6.  Holmes Group. (1986). *Tomorrow's teachers*. East Lansing, MI: Author; Wang, M. C., Haertel, G. D., & Walberg, H. J. (1993). Toward a knowledge base for school learning. *Review of Educational Research, 63*(3), 249–294.

7.  See, for example, Darling-Hammond, L., & Youngs, P. (2002). Defining "highly qualified teachers": What does "scientifically-based research" actually tell us? *Educational Researcher, 31*(9), 13–25; Marzano, R. J., Pickering, D. J., & Pollock, J. E. (2001). *Classroom instruction that works: Research-based strategies for increasing student achievement*. Alexandria, VA: Association for Supervision and Curriculum Development; Stronge, J. H. (2002). *Qualities of effective teachers*. Alexandria, VA: Association for Supervision and Curriculum Development. Also, see, Corcoran, T., & Goertz, M. (1995). Instructional capacity and high-performance schools. *Educational Researcher, 24*, 27–31; Rosenshine, B. (1971). *Teaching behaviors and student achievement*. Windsor, England: National Foundation for Educational Research.

8.  Wang, Haertel, & Walberg, 1993, p. 275.

9.  Wang, Haertel, & Walberg, 1993.

10. Wiggins, G., & McTighe, J. (1998). *Understanding by design*. Alexandria, VA: Association for Supervision and Curriculum Development.

11. Spring, J. (1990). *The American school 1642–1990* (2nd ed.). White Plains, NY: Longman.

12. Spring, 1990.

13. Urban, W., & Wagoner, J. (2000). *American education: A history* (2nd ed.). Boston: McGraw-Hill Higher Education.

14. Coles, A. D. (1999, June 16). Mass-produced pencil leaves its mark. Retrieved February 19, 2004, from www.edweek.org/ew/vol-18/40pencil.h18; Hoff, D. J. (1999, June 16). Made to measure. *Education Week*, 21–27.

15. Coles, 1999.

16. Falk, B. (2000). *The heart of the matter: Using standards and assessment to learn*. Portsmouth, NH: Heinemann, p.4; Urban & Wagoner, 2000, pp. 244–245.

17. Kohn, A. (2000). *The case against standardized testing*. Portsmouth, NH: Heineman.

18. Roderick, M., Jacob, B. A., & Bryk, A. S. (2002). The impact of high-stakes testing in Chicago on student achievement in promotional gate grades. *Educational Evaluation and Policy Analysis, 24*, 333–357, p. 333.

19. Carnoy, M., & Loeb, S. (2002). Does external accountability affect student outcomes: A cross-state analysis. *Educational Evaluation and Policy Analysis, 24*, 305–331, p. 305.

20. Salvia, J., & Ysseldyke, J. E. (1998). *Assessment* (7th ed.). Boston: Houghton Mifflin.

21. Borg, W. R., & Gall, M. D. (1989). *Educational research: An introduction* (5th ed.). New York: Longman, p. 265.

22. Popham, W. J. (2002). *Classroom assessment: What teachers need to know* (3rd ed.). Boston: Allyn and Bacon, p. 364.

23. Borg & Gall, 1989, p. 265.

24. Eisner, E. W. (1999). The uses and limits of performance assessment. *Phi Delta Kappan, 80*, 658–660, p. 659.

25. The descriptions for Oregon, Thompson, CO, and Tennessee are adapted from the article: Tucker, P. D. & Stronge, J. H. (2001). Measure for measure: Using student test results in teacher evaluations. *American School Board Journal, 188*(9), 34–37.

26. Schalock, H. D., Schalock, M. D., & Girod, G. (1997). Teacher work sample methodology as used at Western Oregon State University. In J. Millman (Ed.), *Grading teachers, grading schools: Is student achievement a valid evaluation measure?* (pp. 15–45). Thousand Oaks, CA: Corwin Press, pp. 18–19.

## Chapter 3

1.  Airasian, P. W. (1997). Oregon Teacher Work Sample Methodology: Potential and problems. In J. Millman (Ed.), *Grading teachers, grading schools: Is student achievement a valid evaluation measure?* (pp. 46–52). Thousand Oaks, CA: Corwin Press, p. 47.

2.  All interviews for this chapter were conducted on June 11, 1999. Del Schalock, Teaching Research Division, Western Oregon University, personal interview.

3.  Del Schalock, personal communication, June 11, 1999.

4.  McConney, A. A., Schalock, M. D., & Schalock, H. D. (1998). Focusing improvement and quality assurance: Work samples as authentic performance measures of prospective teachers' effectiveness. *Journal of Personnel Evaluation in Education, 11*, 343–363, p. 345.

5.  McConney, Schalock, & Schalock, 1998, p. 345.

6.  Wolf, K., Lichtenstein, G., & Stevenson, C. (1997). Portfolios in teacher evaluation. In J. H. Stronge (Ed.), *Evaluating teaching: A guide to current thinking and best practice* (pp. 193–214). Thousand Oaks, CA: Corwin Press, p. 193.

7.  McConney, A. A., Schalock, M. D., & Schalock, H. D. (1997). Indicators of student learning in teacher evaluation. In J. H. Stronge (Ed.), *Evaluating teaching: A guide to current thinking and best practice* (pp. 162–192). Thousand Oaks, CA: Corwin Press, p. 173.

8.  McConney, Schalock, & Schalock, 1997, p. 172.

9.  Western Oregon University. (n.d.). *Teacher Effectiveness Project: The reliability and validity of Teacher Work Sample Methodology: A synopsis.* Monmouth, OR: Author, p. 1.

10. Western Oregon University. (n.d.), p. 9.

11. Western Oregon University. (n.d.), pp. 10–11.

12. Schalock, H. D., Schalock, M., & Girod, G. (1997). Teacher Work Sample Methodology as used at Western Oregon State University. In J. Millman (Ed.), *Grading teachers, grading schools: Is student achievement a valid evaluation measure?* (pp. 15–45). Thousand Oaks, CA: Corwin Press, p. 35.

13. Western Oregon University. (n.d.), p. 11.

14. Cowart, B., & Myton, D. (1997). The Oregon Teacher Work Sample Methodology: Rationale and background. In J. Millman (Ed.), *Grading teachers, grading schools: Is student achievement a valid evaluation measure?* (pp. 11–14). Thousand Oaks, CA: Corwin Press, p. 18.

15. Schalock, Schalock, & Girod, 1997, p. 18.

16. Schalock, Schalock, & Girod, 1997, pp. 18–19.

17. Western Oregon University. (n.d.), p. 3.

18. McConney, Schalock, & Schalock, 1997, p. 171.

19. McConney, Schalock, & Schalock, 1997, p. 171.

20. Millman, J. (1981). Student achievement as a measure of teaching competence. In J. Millman (Ed.), *Handbook of teacher evaluation* (pp. 146–166). Beverly Hills, CA: Sage Publications.

21. Schalock, Schalock, & Girod, 1997, pp. 22, 24–25.

22. Our appreciation is extended to Rose Maxey for graciously allowing us to use a Work Sample she developed for a 3rd–4th grade combination class at Washington Elementary School, Salem-Keizer School District (OR), in this illustration.

23. Western Oregon University. (n.d.), p. 3.

24. See Millman, J. (1997). *Grading teachers, grading schools: Is student achievement a valid evaluation measure?* Thousand Oaks, CA: Corwin Press.

25. Schalock, Schalock, & Girod, 1997, p. 36.

26. Susan Wood, Western Oregon University, personal interview.

27. Stufflebeam, D. L. (1997). Oregon Teacher Work Sample Methodology: Educational policy review. In J. Millman (Ed.), *Grading teachers, grading schools: Is student achievement a valid evaluation measure?* (pp. 53–61). Thousand Oaks, CA: Corwin Press, p. 58.

28. James Long, Western Oregon University, personal interview.

29. Sabrina Walker, Western Oregon University, personal interview.

30. Stufflebeam, 1997, p. 59.

31. Del Schalock, Western Oregon University, personal interview.

32. Susan Wood, Western Oregon University, personal interview.

33. James Long, Western Oregon University, personal interview.

34. Darling-Hammond, L. (1997). Toward what end? The evaluation of student learning for the improvement of teaching. In J. Millman (Ed.), *Grading teachers, grading schools: Is student achievement a valid evaluation measure?* (pp. 248–263). Thousand Oaks, CA: Corwin Press, p. 257.
35. Airasian, 1997, p. 47.
36. Robert Ayers, Western Oregon University, personal interview.
37. Rose Maxey, Western Oregon University, personal interview.
38. Airasian, 1997, pp. 49–50.
39. Rose Maxey, Western Oregon University, personal interview.
40. Rose Maxey, Western Oregon University, personal interview.
41. Stufflebeam, 1997, p. 57.
42. Stufflebeam, 1997, p. 58.
43. Airasian, 1997, pp. 49–50.
44. Sabrina Walker, Western Oregon University, personal interview.
45. Schalock, M. D. (1998). Accountability, student learning, and the preparation and licensure of teachers: Oregon's Teacher Work Sample Methodology. *Journal of Personnel Evaluation in Education, 12,* 269–285, p. 279.
46. Schalock, M. D., 1998, p. 279.
47. Schalock, M. D., 1998, p. 280.
48. Schalock, M. D., 1998, p. 283.
49. Stufflebeam, 1997, p. 60.
50. Schalock, Schalock, & Girod, 1997, p. 38.
51. Stufflebeam, 1997, p. 61.
52. Darling-Hammond, 1997b, p. 256.

## Chapter 4

1.  Colorado House Bill 1338, House Bill 1159, and the Colorado Educator Licensing Act.
2.  November, 1995.
3.  All interviews for this chapter were conducted in May, 1999. Interview with John Stewart, Assistant Superintendent of Schools, May, 1999.
4.  Kuzmich, L., & Zila, R. (1998, December). *Developing standards-based professional goals as a focus for teacher evaluation.* Workshop presented at the National Staff Development Council, Washington, DC.
5.  For a discussion of teacher evaluation based on job standards or duties, see: Scriven, M. (1988). Duties-based teacher evaluation. *Journal of Personnel Evaluation in Education, 1,* 319–334. Also see Stronge, J. H. (1997). Improving schools through teacher evaluation. In J. H. Stronge (Ed.), *Evaluating teaching: A guide to current thinking and best practice* (pp. 1–23). Thousand Oaks, CA: Corwin Press.
6.  Thompson School District. (1997–98). Teacher professional standards. *Thompson School District R2-J School Professional Evaluation Handbook.* Loveland, CO: Author, pp. 4–5.
7.  Thompson School District, 1997–98, pp. 4–5.
8.  Kuzmich, L. (1996). Data-driven instruction process. Cited in *Thompson School District school professional evaluation: Toolkit for administrators and school professionals.* Loveland, CO: Author.
9.  Thompson School District. (1996, August). *A parent's guide to standards.* Loveland, CO: Author.
10. Jim Neigherbauer, 6th grade teacher, Thompson School District, personal communication.
11. Lin Kuzmich, elementary school principal, Thompson School District, personal communication.
12. Don Saul, Thompson School Superintendent, Thompson School District, personal communication.

13. Randy Zila, Thompson Director of Human Resources, Thompson School District, personal communication.
14. Jim Willard, Hewlett-Packard executive and Thompson School Board member, personal communication.
15. Jim Neigherbauer, Thompson School District, personal communication.
16. Nancy Popenhagen, Thompson Education Association (NEA) President, personal communication.
17. Lin Kuzmich, Thompson School District, personal communication.
18. Randy Zila, Thompson School District, personal communication.
19. Chris Love, 1st grade teacher, Thompson School District, personal communication.
20. Randy Zila, Thompson School District, personal communication.
21. Jim Willard, Thompson School District, personal communication.
22. Lin Kuzmich, Thompson School District, personal communication.
23. Randy Zila, Thompson School District, personal communication.
24. Don Saul, Thompson School District, personal communication.
25. Chris Love, Thompson School District, personal communication.
26. Don Saul, Thompson School District, personal communication.
27. Jim Willard, Thompson School District, personal communication.
28. Nancy Popenhagen, Thompson School District, personal communication.
29. Jim Neigherbauer, Thompson School District, personal communication.
30. Chris Love, Thompson School District, personal communication.
31. Nancy Popenhagen, Thompson School District, personal communication.
32. Lin Kuzmich, Thompson School District, personal communication.
33. Nancy Popenhagen, Thompson School District, personal communication.
34. Lin Kuzmich, Thompson School District, personal communication.
35. Randy Zila, Thompson School District, personal communication.
36. Chris Love, Thompson School District, personal communication.
37. Nancy Popenhagen, Thompson School District, personal communication.
38. Jim Neigherbauer, Thompson School District, personal communication.
39. Chris Love, Thompson School District, personal communication.

## Chapter 5

1. Alexandria City Public Schools. (2003a). Fast facts: Alexandria City Public Schools at a glance. Retrieved February 15, 2004, from http://www.acps.k12.va.us/fastfact.php
2. Alexandria City Public Schools. (2003b). Proposed operating budget FY 2005: Special needs enrollment. Retrieved February 15, 2004.
http://www.acps.k12.va.us/budgets/op2005_b.pdf
3. Alexandria City Public Schools. (2003c). ACPS food and nutritional services. Retrieved February 15, 2004, from http://www.acps.k12.va.us/fns/stats.pdf
4. Alexandria City Public Schools, 2003a.
5. Alexandria City Public Schools. (2003d). About ACPS. Retrieved February 15, 2004, from http://www.acps.k12.va.us/promo.php
6. Alexandria City Public Schools, 2003a.
7. Alexandria City Public Schools. (2003a); Virginia Department of Education. (2003). Summary FY 2003: Increases in classroom teacher salaries. Retrieved February 25, 2004, from www.pen.k12.va.us/VDOE/Finance/Budget/2002-2003SalarySurvey FinalRptforweb.pdf
8. Alexandria City Public Schools, 2003a.
9. Wilkerson, D., Manatt, R., Rogers, M., & Maughan, R. (2000). Validation of student, principal, and self-ratings in 360-degree feedback for teacher evaluation. *Journal of Personnel Evaluation in Education, 14*(2), 179–192.

10. Wright, S., Horn, S., & Sanders, W. (1997). Teacher and classroom context effects on student achievement: Implications for teacher evaluation. *Journal of Personnel Evaluation in Education, 1*(11), 57–67.
11. Administrator A, personal communication, October 30, 2003.
12. Stronge, J. H. (1997). Improving schools through teacher evaluation. In J. H. Stronge (Ed.), *Evaluating teaching: A guide to current thinking and best practice* (pp. 1–23). Thousand Oaks, CA: Corwin Press.
13. Stronge, J., & Tucker, P. (2000). *Teacher evaluation and student achievement.* Washington, DC: National Education Association, p.53.
14. Alexandria City Public Schools. (2000a). *Teacher evaluation technical manual.* Alexandria, VA: Author, p. 8.
15. Wright et al., 1997.
16. Stronge, 1997.
17. Alexandria City Public Schools, 2000a, p. 28.
18. Alexandria City Public Schools, 2000a, p. 31.
19. Virginia State Department of Education. (2000). *Virginia school laws.* Charlottesville, VA: The Michie Company.
20. Alexandria City Public Schools. (2000b). *Academic goal-setting.* Alexandria, VA: Author, p. 53.
21. Administrator E, personal communication, December 3, 2003.
22. Teacher B, personal communication, November 25, 2003.
23. Administrator B, personal communication, October 30, 2003.
24. Teacher A, personal communication, November 25, 2003.
25. Teacher E, personal communication, December 3, 2003.
26. Teacher B, personal communication, November 25, 2003.
27. Teacher F, personal communication, December 3, 2003.
28. Teacher E, personal communication, December 3, 2003.
29. Administrator C, personal communication, October 30, 2003.
30. Administrator E, personal communication, December 3, 2003.
31. Administrator C, personal communication, October 30, 2003.
32. Teacher F, personal communication, December 3, 2003.
33. Little, J., Gearhart, M., Curry, M., & Kafka, J. (2003). Looking at student work for teacher learning, teacher community, and school reform. *Phi Delta Kappan, 85*(3), 185–192.
34. Teacher B, personal communication, November 25, 2003.
35. Carey, K. (2004). The real value of teachers: Using new information about teacher effectiveness to close the achievement gap. *Thinking K–16, 8*(1), p. 6.
36. Teacher B, personal communication, November 25, 2003.
37. Teacher E, personal communication, December 3, 2003.
38. Administrator E, Personal communication, December 3, 2003.
39. Black, P. & Wiliam, D. (1998). Inside the black box: Raising standards through classroom assessment. *Phi Delta Kappan, 80,* 139–148.
40. Bloom, B. S. (1984). The search for methods of group instruction as effective as one-to-one tutoring. *Educational Leadership, 41*(8), 4–17.
41. Walberg, H. J. (1984). Improving the productivity of America's schools. *Educational Leadership, 41*(8), 19–27.
42. Marzano, R. J., Pickering, D. J., & Pollock, J. E. (2001). *Classroom instruction that works: Research-based strategies for increasing student achievement.* Alexandria, VA: Association for Supervision and Curriculum Development.
43. Marzano, Pickering, & Pollock, 2001, pp. 94–95.
44. Lois Berlin, personal communication, March 10, 2004.
45. Administrator E, personal communication, December 3, 2003.

## Chapter 6

1.  Carey, K. (2004). The real value of teachers: Using new information about teacher effectiveness to close the achievement gap. *Thinking K–16, 8*(1), p. 38.
2.  Sanders, W. L., & Horn, S. P. (1994). The Tennessee Value-Added Assessment System (TVAAS): Mixed-model methodology in educational assessment. *Journal of Personnel Evaluation in Education, 8,* 299–311.
3.  Sanders, W. L., Saxton, A. M., & Horn, S. P. (1997). The Tennessee Value-Added Accountability System: A quantitative, outcomes-based approach to educational assessment. In J. Millman (Ed.), *Grading teachers, grading schools: Is student achievement a valid evaluation measure?* (pp. 137–162). Thousand Oaks, CA: Corwin Press.
4.  Education Improvement Act, 9 Ten. Stat. Ann. §49-1-603-608 (1990 Supp. 1992).
5.  Hill, D. (2000). He's got your number. *Teacher Magazine, 11*(8), 42–47.
6.  Vaughan, A. C. (2002). Standards, accountability, and the determination of school success. *The Educational Forum, 22,* 206–213.
7.  See Sanders & Horn, 1994; Wright, S. P., Horn, S. P., & Sanders, W. L. (1997). Teacher and classroom context effects on student achievement: Implications for teacher evaluation. *Journal of Personnel Evaluation in Education, 11,* 57–67; Sanders, W. L., & Horn, S. P. (1998). Research findings from the Tennessee Value-Added Assessment System (TVAAS) database: Implications for education evaluation and research. *Journal of Personnel Evaluation in Education, 12,* 247–256.
8.  Hill, 2000.
9.  See Dr. William L. Sanders at http://www.sas.com/govedu/education/evaas/bio.html
10. Sanders & Horn, 1994, p. 301.
11. Ceperley, P. E., & Reel, K. (1997). The impetus for the Tennessee Value-Added Accountability System. In J. Millman (Ed.), *Grading teachers, grading schools: Is student achievement a valid evaluation measure?* (pp. 133–136). Thousand Oaks, CA: Corwin Press, pp. 135–136.
12. Ceperley & Reel, 1997.
13. Tennessee Department of Education. (2000). *Framework for Evaluation and Professional Development.* Nashville, TN: Office of Professional Development, p. 7.
14. Tennessee Department of Education, 2000, p. 7.
15. Sanders & Horn, 1998.
16. Sanders, Saxton, & Horn, 1997, p. 141.
17. Ross, S. M., Wang, L. W., Alberg, M., Sanders, W. L., Wright, S. P., & Stringfield, S. (2001, April). *Fourth-year achievement results on the Tennessee Value-Added Assessment System for restructuring schools in Memphis.* Paper presented at the annual meeting of the American Education Research Association, Seattle, WA.
18. Sanders, W. L. (1998). Value-added assessment. *School Administrator, 11*(55), 24–27.
19. Sanders & Horn, 1998.
20. Sanders & Horn, 1998.
21. Sanders & Horn, 1998, p. 250.
22. Sanders, Saxton, & Horn, 1997, p. 139.
23. Sanders & Horn, 1998, p. 251.
24. Darlington, R. B. (1997). The Tennessee Value-Added Assessment System: A challenge to familiar assessment methods. In J. Millman (Ed.), *Grading teachers, grading schools: Is student achievement a valid evaluation measure?* (pp. 163–168). Thousand Oaks, CA: Corwin Press.
25. Wright, Horn, & Sanders, 1997.
26. Wright, Horn, & Sanders, 1997.
27. Stone, J. E. (1999). Value-added assessment: An accountability revolution. In M. Kanstoroom & C. E. Finn, Jr. (Eds.), *Better teachers, better schools.* Washington, DC: Thomas B. Fordham Foundation.
28. Sanders, Saxton, & Horn, 1997.

29. Sanders, Saxton, & Horn, 1997, p. 143.

30. Sanders & Horn, 1998, p. 255.

31. Sanders, 1998.

32. Sanders & Horn, 1994, p. 303.

33. Sanders, W. L., & Horn, S. P. (1995). *An overview of the Tennessee Value-Added Assessment System.* Knoxville, TN: University of Tennessee Value-Added Research and Assessment Center.

34. Until 1999, the CTBS/4 constituted the norm-referenced portion of the test used by TVAAS. In 1999, Tennessee switched to TerraNova.

35. See www.state.tn.us/education/mtest.htm

36. TerraNova is a test developed by McGraw-Hill.

37. Tennessee Department of Education, 2000, p. 10.

38. Tennessee Department of Education, 2000, p. 8.

39. Kupermintz, H. (2003). Teacher effects and teacher effectiveness: A validity investigation of the Tennessee Value-Added Assessment System. *Educational Evaluation and Policy Analysis, 25,* 287–298.

40. Walberg, H. J., & Paik, S. J. (1997). Assessment requires incentives to add value: A review of the Tennessee Value-Added Assessment System. In J. Millman (Ed.), *Grading teachers, grading schools: Is student achievement a valid evaluation measure?* (pp. 169–178). Thousand Oaks, CA: Corwin Press.

41. Walberg & Paik, 1997, p. 171.

42. All interviews for this chapter were conducted in June 1999. Teachers at Carter Elementary School, personal communication.

43. Glenda Russell, math teacher, personal communication.

44. Bratton, S. E., Jr., Horn, S. P., & Wright, S. P. (1996). *Using and interpreting Tennessee's Value-Added Assessment System: A primer for teachers and principal* [Booklet]. Knoxville, TN: University of Tennessee.

45. Bratton, Horn, & Wright, 1996, pp. 26–28.

46. McLean, R. A., & Sanders. W. L. (1984). *Objective component of teacher evaluation: A feasibility study* (Working Paper No. 199). Knoxville: University of Tennessee, College of Business Administration.

47. Sanders, Saxton, & Horn, 1997, p. 161.

48. Kupermintz, 2003.

49. Gary Harman, President of the Knox County Education Association, personal communication, June 1999.

50. Hill, 2000.

51. Gary Harman, President of the Knox County Education Association, personal communication.

52. Bratton, Horn, & Wright, 1996, p. 30.

53. Darling-Hammond, L. (1997b). Toward what end? The evaluation of student learning for the improvement of teaching. In J. Millman (Ed.), *Grading teachers, grading schools: Is student achievement a valid evaluation measure?* (pp. 248–263). Thousand Oaks, CA: Corwin Press, p. 250.

54. Kupermintz, 2003.

55. Bock, R. D., & Wolfe, R. (1996). *A review and analysis of the Tennessee Value-Added Assessment System.* Knoxville, TN: Tennessee Comptroller of the Treasury.

56. Hill, 2000, p. 45.

57. University of Tennessee Value-Added Research and Assessment Center, 1997.

58. See http://evaas.sasinschool.com/evaas/Reports/TVAAS_DistVA.jsp?districtid=470

59. See http://nces.ed.gov/nationsreportcard/states/profile.asp?state=TN

60. Glenda Russell, math teacher, personal communication.

61. Robelen, E. W. (2003, May 7). Tennessee seeks to use student tests to show teacher quality. *Education Week, 22,* 27.

62. Mathews, J. (2004, February 10). A move to invest more in effective teaching. *The Washington Post*, p. A10.
63. Olson, L. (2004, March 3). Tennessee reconsiders Value-Added Assessment System. *Education Week*, p. 9.
64. Carey, 2004, p. 5.
65. Glenda Russell, math teacher, personal communication.
66. Mathews, J. (2000, March 14). Testing students, scoring teachers. *The Washington Post*, p. A7.
67. Hill, 2000.
68. Teachers at Carter Elementary School, personal communication.
69. Hill, 2000.
70. Archer, J. (1999, May 5). Sanders 101. *Education Week*, pp.26–28, p. 27.
71. Rick Privette, Principal at Carter Elementary School in Knox County, personal communication.
72. Sanders, Saxton, & Horn, 1997.
73. Hill, 2000, p. 42.
74. Sanders & Horn, 1994, p. 301.

## Chapter 7

1. Darling-Hammond, L. (1997). *The right to learn: A blueprint for creating schools that work*. San Francisco: Jossey-Bass.
2. Cowart, B., & Myton, D. (1997). The Oregon Teacher Work Sample Methodology: Rationale and background. In J. Millman (Ed.) *Grading teachers, grading schools: Is student achievement a valid evaluation measure?* p. 11, Thousand Oaks, CA: Corwin Press.
3. See *The Personnel Evaluation Standards* (1988) by the Joint Committee on Standards for Educational Evaluation. Newbury Park, CA: Corwin Press.
4. Wright, S. P., Horn, S. P., & Sanders, W. L. (1997). Teacher and classroom context effects on student achievement: Implications for teacher evaluation. *Journal of Personnel Evaluation in Education, 11*, 57–67, p. 61.
5. Wright, Horn, & Sanders, 1997, p. 66.
6. Popham, W. J. (1999). Why standardized tests don't measure educational quality. *Educational Leadership, 56*(6), 8–15.
7. Resnick, L. B. (1999, June 16). Making America smarter. *Education Week*, 38–40.
8. Wheeler, P. H. (1995). Before you use student tests in teacher evaluation . . . consider these issues. *AASPA Report*. Virginia Beach, VA: American Association of School Personnel Administrators.
9. Wright, Horn, & Sanders, 1997, p. 66.
10. Viader, D., & Blair, J. (1999, September 29). Error affects test results in six states. *Education Week*, 1, 13–15.
11. Viader & Blair, 1999.
12. Wheeler, 1995.
13. McConney, A. A., Schalock, M. D., & Schalock, H. D. (1997). Indicators of student learning in teacher evaluation. In J. H. Stronge (Ed.) *Evaluating teaching: A guide to current thinking and best practice* (pages 162–192). Thousand Oaks, CA: Corwin Press.
14. See, for example, Haertel, E. (1986). The valid use of student performance measures for teacher evaluation. *Educational Evaluation and Policy Analysis, 8*, 45–60.
15. McConney, Schalock, & Schalock, 1997, p. 177. Curricular validity, a second aspect of validity that should be considered in settings such as proposed here, is discussed later in the chapter.
16. Perfect consistency is rarely achieved, so an *acceptable* level of reliability, in measures such as inter-rater reliability, should be considered.
17. McConney, Schalock, & Schalock, 1997, p. 178.
18. McConney, Schalock, & Schalock, 1997, p. 177.

## Appendix A

1. Darling-Hammond, L. (2000). Teacher quality and student achievement: A review of state policy evidence. *Education Policy Analysis Archives, 8*(1). Retrieved January 22, 2004, from http://olam.ed.asu.edu/epaa/v8n1/; Haberman, M. (1995). *STAR teachers of children in poverty*. West Lafayette, IN: Kappa Delta Phi; Hanushek, E. (1971). Teacher characteristics and gains in student achievement: Estimation using micro data. *American Economic Review, 61*(2), 280–288.
2. Darling-Hammond, L. (2001). The challenge of staffing our schools. *Educational Leadership, 58*(8), 12–17; Ehrenberg, R. G., & Brewer, D. J. (1995). Did teachers' verbal ability and race matter in the 1960's? Coleman revisited. *Economics of Educational Review, 14*(1), 1–21; Gitomer, D. H., Latham, A. S., & Ziomek, R. (1999). *The academic quality of prospective teachers: The impact of admissions and licensure testing.* Retrieved from http://www.ets.org/research/dload/225033.pdf; Greenwald, R., Hedges, L., & Laine, R. (1996). The effect of school resources on student achievement. *Review of Education Research, 66*(3), 361–396; Strauss, R. P., & Sawyer, E. A. (1986). Some new evidence on teacher and student competencies. *Economics of Education Review, 5*(1), 41–48; Wayne, A. J., & Youngs, P. (2003). Teacher characteristics and student achievement gains: A review. *Review of Educational Research, 73*(1), 89–122.
3. Fetler, M. (1999). High school staff characteristics and mathematics test results. *Educational Policy Analysis Archives, 7*(9). Retrieved from http://olam.ed.asu.edu/v7n9; Langer, J. (2001). Beating the odds: Teaching middle and high school students to read and write well. *American Educational Research Journal, 38*(4), 837–880; Wenglinsky, H. (2000). *How teaching matters: Bringing the classroom back into discussions of teacher quality.* Princeton, NJ: Millikan Family Foundation and Educational Testing Service.
4. Popham, W. J. (1999). Why standardized tests don't measure educational quality. *Educational Leadership, 56*(6), 8–15.
5. Camphire, G. (2001). Are our teachers good enough? *SED Letter, 13*(2). Retrieved November 12, 2001, from http://www.sedl.org/pubs/sedletter/v13n2/1.htm; Cross, C., & Regden, D. W. (2002). Improving teacher quality. *American School Board Journal.* Retrieved May 17, 2002, from http://www.absj.com/current/coverstory2.html
6. Darling-Hammond, 2000; Darling-Hammond, 2001; Goldhaber, D. D., & Brewer, D. J. (2000). Does teacher certification matter? High school teacher certification status and student achievement. *Educational Evaluation and Policy Analysis, 22*(2), 129–145; Hawk, P. P., Coble, C. R., & Swanson, M. (1985). Certification: Does it matter? *Journal of Teacher Education, 36*(3), 13–15; Laczko-Kerr, I., & Berliner, D.C. (2002, September 6). The effectiveness of "Teach for America" and other under-certified teachers on student academic achievement: A case of harmful public policy. *Education Policy Analysis Archives, 10*(37). Retrieved November 4, 2003, from http://epaa.asu.edu/epaa/v10n37/
7. Darling-Hammond, 2001; Hawk et al., 1985; Wayne, A. J., & Youngs, P. (2003). Teacher characteristics and student achievement gains: A review. *Review of Educational Research, 73*(1), 89–122.
8. Sanders, W. L. (2001, January). *The effect of teachers on student achievement.* Keynote address at the Project STARS Institute, Williamsburg, VA; Scherer, M. (2001). Improving the quality of the teaching force: A conversation with David C. Berliner. *Educational Leadership, 58*(8), 6–10.
9. Darling-Hammond, 2001; Sanders, 2001.
10. Cruickshank, D. R., & Haefele, D. (2001). Good teachers, plural. *Educational Leadership, 58*(5), 26–30; Johnson, B. L. (1997). An organizational analysis of multiple perspectives of effective teaching: Implications for teacher evaluation. *Journal of Personnel Evaluation in Education, 11,* 69-87; Peart, N. A., & Campbell, F. A. (1999). At-risk students' perceptions of teacher effectiveness. *Journal for a Just and Caring Education, 5*(3), 269–284; Thomas, J. A., & Montomery, P. (1998). On becoming a good teacher:

Reflective practice with regard to children's voices. *Journal of Teacher Education, 49*(5), 372–380.

11. Kohn, A. (1996). What to look for in a classroom. *Educational Leadership, (54)*1, 54–55.

12. Collinson, V., Killeavy, M., & Stephenson, H. J. (1999). Exemplary teachers: Practicing an ethic of care in England, Ireland, and the United States. *Journal for a Just and Caring Education, 5*(4), 349–366; Deiro, J. A. (2003). Do your students know you care? *Educational Leadership, 60*(6), 60–62; Ford, D. Y., & Trotman, M. F. (2001). Teachers of gifted students: Suggested multicultural characteristics and competencies. *Roper Review, 23*(4), 235–239; Peart & Campbell, 1999; Thomas & Montomery, 1998.

13. Peart & Campbell, 1999.

14. Cruickshank & Haefele, 2001; Ford & Trotman, 2001; Peart & Campbell, 1999; Wolk, S. (2002). *Being good: Rethinking classroom management and student discipline.* Portsmouth, NH: Heinemann.

15. Covino, E. A., & Iwanicki, E. (1996). Experienced teachers: Their constructs on effective teaching. *Journal of Personnel Evaluation in Education, 11*, 325–363.

16. Northwest Regional Educational Laboratory. (2001). *Understanding motivation and supporting teacher renewal.* Retrieved on October 20, 2003, from http://www.nwrel.org/nwreport/jan03/motivation.html

17. Cawelti, G. (1999). *Portraits of six benchmark schools: Diverse approaches to improving student achievement.* Arlington, VA: Educational Research Service.

18. Kerrins, J. A., & Cushing, K.S. (1998, April). *Taking a second look: Expert and novice differences when observing the same classroom teaching segment a second time.* Paper presented at the annual meeting of the American Educational Research Association, San Diego, CA.

19. Grossman, P., Valencia, S., Evans, K., Thompson, C., Martin, S., & Place, N. (2000). *Transitions into teaching: Learning to teach writing in teacher education and beyond.* Retrieved on November 11, 2003, from http://cela.albany.edu/transitions/main.html; Harris, S. (2003). An andragogical model: Learning through life experiences. *Kappa Delta Pi Record, 40*(1), 38–41; Thomas & Montomery, 1998.

20. Emmer, E. T., Evertson, C. M., & Anderson, L. M. (1980). Effective classroom management at the beginning of the school year. *The Elementary School Journal, 80*(5), 219–231; McLeod, J., Fisher, J., & Hoover, G. (2003). *The key elements of classroom management: Managing time and space, student behavior, and instructional strategies.* Alexandria, VA: Association for Supervision and Curriculum Development.

21. Marzano, R. J. (with Marzano, J. S., & Pickering, D. J.). (2003). *Classroom management that works.* Alexandria, VA: Association for Supervision and Curriculum Development.

22. Covino & Iwanicki, 1996; McLeod et al., 2003; Shellard, E., & Protheroe, N. (2000). Effective teaching: How do we know it when we see it? *The Informed Educator Series.* Arlington, VA: Educational Research Services.

23. Johnson, 1997.

24. Thompson, J. G. (2002). *First-year teacher's survival kit.* San Francisco, CA: Jossey-Bass.

25. McLeod et al., 2003; Stronge, J. H., Tucker, P. D., & Ward, T. J. (2003, April). *Teacher effectiveness and student learning: What do good teachers do?* Paper presented at the annual meeting of the American Educational Research Association, Chicago, IL.

26. Kohn, 1996.

27. Covino & Iwanicki, 1996; Peart & Campbell, 1999; Shellard & Protheroe, 2000; Wharton-McDonald, R., Pressley, M., & Hampston, J. M. (1998). Literacy instruction in nine first-grade classrooms: Teacher characteristics and student achievement [Electronic version]. *The Elementary School Journal, 99*(2). Retrieved on October 30, 2003, from http://80-web3.infotrac.galegroup.com.proxy.wm.edu/itw/infomark/993/701/64058160w3/purl=rc1_EAIM_0_A54851458&dyn=4!ar_fmt?sw_aep=viva_wm

28. Cruickshank & Haefele, 2001; Emmer, Evertson, & Anderson, 1980.

29. Bransford, J. D., Brown, A. L., & Cocking, R. R. (Eds.). (1999). *How people learn: Brain, mind, experience, and school.* Washington, DC: National Academy Press; Jackson, A. W., & Davis, G. A. (with Abeel, M., & Bordonard, A.). (2000). *Turning points 2000: Educating adolescents in the 21st Century.* New York: Teachers College Press; Panasuk, R., Stone, W., & Todd, J. (2002). Lesson planning strategy for effective mathematics teaching. *Education, 22*(2), 714, 808–827.

30. Bloom, B. S. (1984). The search for methods of group instruction as effective as one-to-one tutoring. *Educational Leadership, 41*(8), 4–17; Zahorik, J., Halbach, A., Ehrle, K., & Molnar, A. (2003). Teaching practices for smaller classes. *Educational Leadership, 61*(1), 75–77.

31. Covino & Iwanicki, 1996; Wenglinsky, 2000.

32. Covino & Iwanicki, 1996.

33. Gamoran, A., & Nystrand, M. (1992). Taking students seriously. In F. M. Newmann (Ed.), *Student engagement and achievement in American secondary schools.* New York: Teachers College Press.

34. Martin, R., Sexton, C., & Gerlovich, J. (2001). *Teaching science for all children* (3rd ed.). Boston: Allyn and Bacon.

35. Collinson, Killeavy, & Stephenson, 1999; Corno, L. (2000). Looking at homework differently. *The Elementary School Journal, 100*(5), 529–549; Covino & Iwanicki, 1996; Wenglinsky, 2000.

36. Bloom, 1984; Darling-Hammond, 2001; Johnson, 1997; Langer, 2001; Sanders, W. L., & Horn, S. P. (1998). Research findings from the Tennessee Value-Added Assessment System (TVAAS) database: Implications for educational evaluation and research. *Journal of Personnel Evaluation in Education, 12*, 247–256; Skrla, L. (2001). The influence of state accountability on teacher expectations and student performance. *UCEA: The Review, 42*(2), 1–4; Wenglinsky, 2000; Tomlinson, C. A. (1999). *The differentiated classroom: Responding to the needs of all learners.* Alexandria, VA: Association for Supervision and Curriculum Development.

37. Covino & Iwanicki, 1996.

38. Marzano, R. J., Pickering, D. J., & McTighe, J. (1993). *Assessing student outcomes: Performance assessment using the dimensions of learning model.* Alexandria, VA: Association for Supervision and Curriculum Development.

39. Emmer, E. T., Evertson, C. M., & Anderson, L. M. (1980). Effective classroom management at the beginning of the school year. *The Elementary School Journal, 80*(5), 219–231.

40. Covino & Iwanicki, 1996.

41. Stronge, Tucker, & Ward, 2003.

42. Cotton, K. (2000). *The schooling practices that matter most.* Portland, OR: Northwest Regional Educational Laboratory, and Alexandria, VA: Association for Supervision and Curriculum Development; Marzano, R. J., Norford, J. S., Paynter, D. E., Pickering, D. J., & Gaddy, B. B. (2001). *A handbook for classroom instruction that works.* Alexandria, VA: Association for Supervision and Curriculum Development; Walberg, H. J. (1984). Improving the productive of America's schools. *Educational Leadership, 41*(8), 19–27.

# Bibliography

Airasian, P. W. (1997). Oregon Teacher Work Sample Methodology: Potential and problems. In J. Millman (Ed.), *Grading teachers, grading schools: Is student achievement a valid evaluation measure?* (pp. 46–52). Thousand Oaks, CA: Corwin Press.

Alexandria City Public Schools. (2000a). *Teacher evaluation technical manual.* Alexandria, VA: Author.

Alexandria City Public Schools. (2000b). *Academic goal setting.* Alexandria, VA: Author.

Alexandria City Public Schools. (2003a). Fast facts: Alexandria City Public Schools at a glance. Retrieved February 15, 2004, from http://www.acps.k12.va.us/fastfact.php

Alexandria City Public Schools. (2003b). Proposed operating budget FY 2005: Special needs enrollment. Retrieved February 15, 2004, http://www.acps.k12.va.us/budgets/op2005_b.pdf

Alexandria City Public Schools. (2003c). ACPS food and nutritional services. Retrieved February 15, 2004, from http://www.acps.k12.va.us/fns/stats.pdf

Alexandria City Public Schools. (2003d). About ACPS. Retrieved February 15, 2004, from http://www.acps.k12.va.us/promo.php

Archer, J. (1999, May 5). Sanders 101. *Education Week,* 26–28.

Bearden, D. K., Bembry, K. L., & Babu, S. (1995, April). *Effective schools: Is there a winning combination of administrators, teachers, and students?* Paper presented at the annual meeting of the American Educational Research Association, San Francisco, CA.

Bembry, K., Jordan, H., Gomez, E., Anderson, M., & Mendro, R. (1998, April). *Policy implications of long-term teacher effects on student achievement.* Paper presented at the annual meeting of the American Educational Research Association, San Diego, CA.

Black, P., & Wiliam, D. (1998). Inside the black box: Raising standards through classroom assessment. *Phi Delta Kappan, 80,* 139–148.

Bloom, B. S. (1984). The search for methods of group instruction as effective as one-to-one tutoring. *Educational Leadership, 41*(8), 4–17.

Bock, R. D., & Wolfe, R. (1996). *A review and analysis of the Tennessee Value-Added Assessment System.* Knoxville, TN: Tennessee Comptroller of the Treasury.

Borg, W. R., & Gall, M. D. (1989). *Educational research: An introduction* (5th Ed.). New York: Longman.

Bransford, J. D., Brown, A. L., & Cocking, R. R. (Eds.). (1999). *How people learn: Brain, mind, experience, and school*. Washington, DC: National Academy Press.

Bratton, S. E., Jr., Horn, S. P., & Wright, S. P. (1996). *Using and interpreting Tennessee's Value-Added Assessment System: A primer for teachers and principal* [Booklet]. Knoxville, TN: University of Tennessee.

Brophy, J., & Good, T. (1986). Teacher behavior and student achievement. In M. C. Wittrock (Ed.), *Handbook of Research on Teaching* (pp. 328–375). New York: MacMillan.

Camphire, G. (2001). Are our teachers good enough? *SED Letter, 13*(2). Retrieved November 12, 2001, from http://www.sedl.org/pubs/sedletter/v13n2/1.htm

Carey, K. (2004). The real value of teachers: Using new information about teacher effectiveness to close the achievement gap. *Thinking K–16, 8*(1), 1–6.

Carnoy, M., & Loeb, S. (2002). Does external accountability affect student outcomes: A cross-state analysis. *Educational Evaluation and Policy Analysis, 24*, 305–331.

Cawelti, G. (1999). *Portraits of six benchmark schools: Diverse approaches to improving student achievement*. Arlington, VA: Educational Research Service.

Ceperley, P. E., & Reel, K. (1997). The impetus for the Tennessee Value-Added Accountability System. In J. Millman (Ed.), *Grading teachers, grading schools: Is student achievement a valid evaluation measure?* (pp. 133–136). Thousand Oaks, CA: Corwin Press.

Coles, A. D. (1999, June 16). Mass-produced pencil leaves its mark. Retrieved February 19, 2004, from www.edweek.org/ew/vol-18/40pencil.h18

Collinson, V., Killeavy, M., & Stephenson, H. J. (1999). Exemplary teachers: Practicing an ethic of care in England, Ireland, and the United States. *Journal for a Just and Caring Education, 5*(4), 349–366.

Colorado Educator Licensing Act (Colo. Rev. Stat., Section 22-60).

Colorado State Legislature HB1338.

Colorado State Legislature HB00-1159.

Corcoran, T., & Goertz, M. (1995). Instructional capacity and high performance schools. *Educational Researcher, 24*, 27–31.

Corno, L. (2000). Looking at homework differently. *The Elementary School Journal, 100*(5), 529–549.

Cotton, K. (2000). *The schooling practices that matter most*. Portland, OR: Northwest Regional Educational Laboratory, and Alexandria, VA: Association for Supervision and Curriculum Development.

Covino, E. A., & Iwanicki, E. (1996). Experienced teachers: Their constructs on effective teaching. *Journal of Personnel Evaluation in Education, 11*, 325–363.

Cowart, B., & Myton, D. (1997). The Oregon Teacher Work Sample Methodology: Rationale and background. In J. Millman (Ed.), *Grading teachers, grading schools: Is student achievement a valid evaluation measure?* (pp. 11–14). Thousand Oaks, CA: Corwin Press.

Cross, C., & Regden, D. W. (2002). Improving teacher quality. *American School Board Journal*. Retrieved May 17, 2002, from http://www.absj.com/current/coverstory2.html

Cruickshank, D. R., & Haefele, D. (2001). Good teachers, plural. *Educational Leadership, 58*(5), 26–30.

Cunningham, L. L. (1997). In the beginning. In J. Millman (Ed.), *Grading teachers, grading schools: Is student achievement a valid evaluation measure?* Thousand Oaks, CA: Corwin Press.

Danielson, C. (1996). *Enhancing professional practice: A framework for teaching*. Alexandria, VA: Association for Supervision and Curriculum Development.

Darling-Hammond, L. (1997a). *The right to learn: A blueprint for creating schools that work*. San Francisco: Jossey-Bass.

Darling-Hammond, L. (1997b). Toward what end? The evaluation of student learning for the improvement of teaching. In J. Millman (Ed.), *Grading teachers, grading schools: Is student achievement a valid evaluation measure?* (pp. 248–263). Thousand Oaks, CA: Corwin Press.

Darling-Hammond, L. (2000). Teacher quality and student achievement: A review of state policy evidence. *Education Policy Analysis Archives, 8*(1). Retrieved January 22, 2004, from http://olam.ed.asu.edu/epaa/v8n1/

Darling-Hammond, L. (2001). The challenge of staffing our schools. *Educational Leadership, 58*(8), 12–17.

Darling-Hammond, L., & Youngs, P. (2002). Defining "highly qualified teachers": What does "scientifically-based research" actually tell us? *Educational Researcher, 31*(9), 13–25.

Darlington, R. B. (1997). The Tennessee Value-Added Assessment System: A challenge to familiar assessment methods. In J. Millman (Ed.), *Grading teachers, grading schools: Is student achievement a valid evaluation measure?* (pp. 163–168). Thousand Oaks, CA: Corwin Press.

Deiro, J. A. (2003). Do your students know you care? *Educational Leadership, 60*(6), 60–62.

Duke, D. L. (1990). Developing teacher evaluation systems that promote professional growth. *Journal of Personnel Evaluation in Education, 4*, 131–144.

Education Improvement Act, 9 Ten. Stat. Ann. ß49-1-603-608 (1990 Supp. 1992).

Educational Research Service. (1988). *Teacher evaluation: Practices and procedures.* Arlington, VA: Author.

Ehrenberg, R. G., & Brewer, D. J. (1995). Did teachers' verbal ability and race matter in the 1960's? Coleman revisited. *Economics of Educational Review, 14*(1), 1–21.

Eisner, E. W. (1999). The uses and limits of performance assessment. *Phi Delta Kappan, 80*, 658–660.

Emmer, E. T., Evertson, C. M., & Anderson, L. M. (1980). Effective classroom management at the beginning of the school year. *The Elementary School Journal, 80*(5), 219–231.

Falk, B. (2000). *The heart of the matter: Using standards and assessment to learn.* Portsmouth, NH: Heinemann.

Fetler, M. (1999). High school staff characteristics and mathematics test results. *Educational Policy Analysis Archives, 7*(9). Retrieved from http://olam.ed.asu.edu/v7n9

Ford, D. Y., & Trotman, M. F. (2001). Teachers of gifted students: Suggested multicultural characteristics and competencies. *Roper Review, 23*(4), 235–239.

Frymier, J. (1998). Accountability and student learning. *Journal of Personnel Evaluation in Education, 12*, 233–235.

Gamoran, A., & Nystrand, M. (1992). Taking students seriously. In F. M. Newmann (Ed.), *Student engagement and achievement in American secondary schools.* New York: Teachers College Press.

Gitomer, D. H., Latham, A. S., & Ziomek, R. (1999). *The academic quality of prospective teachers: The impact of admissions and licensure testing.* Retrieved from http://www.ets.org/research/dload/225033.pdf

Goldhaber, D. D., & Brewer, D. J. (2000). Does teacher certification matter? High school teacher certification status and student achievement. *Educational Evaluation and Policy Analysis, 22*(2), 129–145.

Greenwald, R., Hedges, L., & Laine, R. (1996). The effect of school resources on student achievement. *Review of Education Research, 66*(3), 361–396.

Grossman, P., Valencia, S., Evans, K., Thompson, C., Martin, S., & Place, N. (2000). *Transitions into teaching: Learning to teach writing in teacher education and beyond.* Retrieved on November 11, 2003, from http://cela.albany.edu/transitions/main.html

Haberman, M. (1995). *STAR teachers of children in poverty.* West Lafayette, IN: Kappa Delta Phi.

Hanushek, E. (1971). Teacher characteristics and gains in student achievement: Estimation using micro data. *American Economic Review, 61*(2), 280-288.

Harris, S. (2003). An andragogical model: Learning through life experiences. *Kappa Delta Pi Record, 40*(1), 38–41.

Hawk, P. P., Coble, C. R., & Swanson, M. (1985). Certification: Does it matter? *Journal of Teacher Education, 36*(3), 13–15.

Hill, D. (2000). He's got your number. *Teacher Magazine, 11*(8), 42–47.

Hoff, D. J. (1999, June 16). Made to measure. *Education Week, 21–27.*

Holmes Group. (1986). *Tomorrow's teachers.* East Lansing, MI: Author.

Howard, B. B., & McColskey, W. H. (2001). Evaluating experienced teachers. *Educational Leadership, 58*(5), 48–51.

Iwanicki, E. F. (1990). Teacher evaluation for school improvement. In J. Millman and L. Darling-Hammond (Eds.), *The new handbook of teacher evaluation: Assessing elementary and secondary school teachers* (pp. 158–171). Newbury Park, CA: Sage Publications.

Jackson, A. W., & Davis, G. A. (with Abeel, M., & Bordonard, A. (2000). *Turning points 2000: Educating adolescents in the 21st century.* New York: Teachers College Press.

Johnson, B. L. (1997). An organizational analysis of multiple perspectives of effective teaching: Implications for teacher evaluation. *Journal of Personnel Evaluation in Education, 11,* 69–87.

Joint Committee on Standards for Educational Evaluation. (1988). *The personnel evaluation standards.* Newbury Park, CA: Corwin Press.

Jordan, H., Mendro, R., & Weerasinghe, D. (1997, July). *Teacher effects on longitudinal student achievement.* Paper presented at the Sixth Annual Evaluation Institute sponsored by CREATE, Indianapolis, IN.

Kerrins, J. A., & Cushing, K. S., (1998, April). *Taking a second look: Expert and novice differences when observing the same classroom teaching segment a second time.* Paper presented at the annual meeting of the American Educational Research Association, San Diego, CA.

Kohn, A. (1996). What to look for in a classroom. *Educational Leadership,* (54)1, 54–55.

Kohn, A. (2000). *The case against standardized testing.* Portsmouth, NH: Heineman.

Kupermintz, H. (2003). Teacher effects and teacher effectiveness: A validity investigation of the Tennessee Value-Added Assessment System. *Educational Evaluation and Policy Analysis, 25,* 287–298.

Kuzmich, L. (1996). Data-driven instruction process. Cited in *Thompson School District school professional evaluation: Toolkit for administrators and school professionals.* Loveland, CO: Author.

Kuzmich, L., & Zila, R. (1998, December). *Developing standards-based professional goals as a focus for teacher evaluation.* Workshop presented at the annual conference of the National Staff Development Council, Washington, DC.

Laczko-Kerr, I., & Berliner, D.C. (2002, September 6). The effectiveness of "Teach for America" and other under-certified teachers on student academic achievement: A case of harmful public policy. *Education Policy Analysis Archives, 10*(37). Retrieved November 4, 2003, from http://epaa.asu.edu/epaa/v10n37/

Langer, J. (2001). Beating the odds: Teaching middle and high school students to read and write well. *American Educational Research Journal, 38*(4), 837–880.

Little, J., Gearhart, M., Curry, M., & Kafka, J. (2003). Looking at student work for teacher learning, teacher community, and school reform. *Phi Delta Kappan, 85*(3), 185–192.

Lortie, D. C. (1975). *School-teacher: A sociological study.* Chicago: University of Chicago Press.

Martin, R., Sexton, C., & Gerlovich, J. (2001). *Teaching science for all children* (3rd Ed.). Boston: Allyn and Bacon.

Marzano, R. J. (with Marzano, J. S., & Pickering, D. J.). (2003). *Classroom management that works.* Alexandria, VA: Association for Supervision and Curriculum Development.

Marzano, R. J., Norford, J. S., Paynter, D. E., Pickering, D. J., & Gaddy, B. B. (2001). *A handbook for classroom instruction that works.* Alexandria, VA: Association for Supervision and Curriculum Development.

Marzano, R. J., Pickering, D., & McTighe, J. (1993). *Assessing student outcomes: Performance assessment using the dimensions of learning model.* Alexandria, VA: Association for Supervision and Curriculum Development.

Marzano, R. J., Pickering, D. J., & Pollock, J. E. (2001). *Classroom instruction that works: Research-based strategies for increasing student achievement.* Alexandria, VA: Association for Supervision and Curriculum Development.

Mathews, J. (2000, March 14). Testing students, scoring teachers. *The Washington Post*, p. A7.

Mathews, J. (2004, February 10). A move to invest more in effective teaching. *The Washington Post*, p. A10.

McConney, A. A., Schalock, M. D., & Schalock, H. D. (1997). Indicators of student learning in teacher evaluation. In J. H. Stronge (Ed.), *Evaluating teaching: A guide to current thinking and best practice* (pp. 162–192). Thousand Oaks, CA: Corwin Press.

McConney, A. A., Schalock, M. D., & Schalock, H. D. (1998). Focusing improvement and quality assurance: Work samples as authentic performance measures of prospective teachers' effectiveness. *Journal of Personnel Evaluation in Education, 11*, 343–363.

McGahie, W. C. (1991). Professional competence evaluation. *Educational Researcher, 20*, 3–9.

McLaughlin, M. W., & Pfeiffer, R. S. (1988). *Teacher evaluation: Improvement, accountability, and effective learning.* New York: Teachers College Press.

McLean, R. A., & Sanders. W. L. (1984). *Objective component of teacher evaluation: A feasibility study* (Working Paper No. 199). Knoxville, TN: University of Tennessee, College of Business Administration.

McLeod, J., Fisher, J., & Hoover, G. (2003). *The key elements of classroom management: Managing time and space, student behavior, and instructional strategies.* Alexandria, VA: Association for Supervision and Curriculum Development.

Medley, D. M., Coker, H., & Soar, R. S. (1984). *Measurement-based evaluation of teacher performance.* New York: Longman.

Mendro, R. L. (1998). Student achievement and school and teacher accountability. *Journal of Personnel Evaluation in Education, 12*, 257–267.

Millman, J. (1981). Student achievement as a measure of teaching competence. In J. Millman (Ed.), *Handbook of teacher evaluation* (pp. 146–166). Beverly Hills, CA: Sage Publications.

Millman, J. (1997). *Grading teachers, grading schools: Is student achievement a valid evaluation measure?* Thousand Oaks, CA: Corwin Press.

National Board for Professional Teaching Standards. (1989). *Toward high and rigorous standards for the teaching profession.* Washington, DC: Author.

National Commission on Teaching and America's Future. (1996). *What matters most: Teaching for America's future.* New York: Author.

Northwest Regional Educational Laboratory. (2001). *Understanding motivation and supporting teacher renewal.* Retrieved on October 20, 2003, from http://www.nwrel.org/nwreport/jan03/motivation.html

Olson, L. (2004, March 3). Tennessee reconsiders Value-Added Assessment System. *Education Week*, p. 9.

Panasuk, R., Stone, W., & Todd, J. (2002). Lesson planning strategy for effective mathematics teaching. *Education, 22*(2), 714, 808–827.

Peart, N. A., & Campbell, F. A. (1999). At-risk students' perceptions of teacher effectiveness. *Journal for a Just and Caring Education, 5*(3), 269–284.

Popham, W. J. (1999). Why standardized tests don't measure educational quality. *Educational Leadership, 56*(6), 8–15.

Popham, W. J. (2002). *Classroom assessment: What teachers need to know* (3rd ed.). Boston: Allyn and Bacon.

Resnick, L. B. (1999, June 16). Making America smarter. *Education Week*, 38–40.

Robelen, E. W. (2003, May 7). Tennessee seeks to use student tests to show teacher quality. *Education Week, 22*, p. 27.

Roderick, M., Jacob, B. A., & Bryk, A. S. (2002). The impact of high-stakes testing in Chicago on student achievement in promotional gate grades. *Educational Evaluation and Policy Analysis, 24*, 333–357.

Rosenshine, B. (1971). *Teaching behaviors and student achievement.* Windsor, England: National Foundation for Educational Research.

Ross, S. M., Wang, L. W., Alberg, M., Sanders, W. L., Wright, S. P., & Stringfield, S. (2001, April). *Fourth-year achievement results on the Tennessee Value-Added Assessment System for restructuring schools in Memphis*. Paper presented at the annual meeting of the American Education Research Association, Seattle, WA.

Salvia, J., & Ysseldyke, J. E. (1998). *Assessment* (7th ed.). Boston: Houghton Mifflin.

Sanders, W. L. (1998). Value-added assessment. *School Administrator, 11*(55), 24–27.

Sanders, W. L. (2001, January). *The effect of teachers on student achievement*. Keynote address at the Project STARS Institute, Williamsburg, VA.

Sanders, W. L., & Horn, S. P. (1994). The Tennessee Value-Added Assessment System (TVAAS): Mixed-model methodology in educational assessment. *Journal of Personnel Evaluation in Education, 8*, 299–311.

Sanders, W. L., & Horn, S. P. (1995). *An overview of the Tennessee Value-Added Assessment System*. Knoxville, TN: University of Tennessee Value-Added Research and Assessment Center.

Sanders, W. L., & Horn, S. P. (1998). Research findings from the Tennessee Value-Added Assessment System (TVAAS) database: Implications for educational evaluation and research. *Journal of Personnel Evaluation in Education, 12*, 247–256.

Sanders, W. L., & Rivers, J. C. (1996). *Cumulative and residual effects of teachers on future student academic achievement* (Research Progress Report). Knoxville, TN: University of Tennessee Value-Added Research and Assessment Center.

Sanders, W. L., Saxton, A. M., & Horn, S. P. (1997). The Tennessee Value-Added Accountability System: A quantitative, outcomes-based approach to educational assessment. In J. Millman (Ed.), *Grading teachers, grading schools: Is student achievement a valid evaluation measure?* (pp. 137–162). Thousand Oaks, CA: Corwin Press.

Schalock, H. D. (1998). Student progress in learning: Teacher responsibility, accountability and reality. *Journal of Personnel Evaluation in Education, 12*(3), 237–246.

Schalock, H. D., Schalock, M., & Girod, G. (1997). Teacher Work Sample Methodology as used at Western Oregon State University. In J. Millman (Ed.), *Grading teachers, grading schools: Is student achievement a valid evaluation measure?* (pp. 15–45). Thousand Oaks, CA: Corwin Press.

Schalock, M. D. (1998). Accountability, student learning, and the preparation and licensure of teachers: Oregon's Teacher Work Sample Methodology. *Journal of Personnel Evaluation in Education, 12*, 269–285.

Scherer, M. (2001). Improving the quality of the teaching force: A conversation with David C. Berliner. *Educational Leadership, 58*(8), 6–10.

Schmoker, M. (1999). *Results: The key to continuous school improvement*. Alexandria, VA: Association for Supervision and Curriculum Development.

Schmoker, M. (2001). *The results handbook*. Alexandria, VA: Association for Supervision and Curriculum Development.

Scriven, M. (1988). Duties-based teacher evaluation. *Journal of Personnel Evaluation in Education, 1*, 319–334.

Scriven, M. (1994). Duties of the teacher. *Journal of Personnel Evaluation in Education, 8*, 151–184.

Shellard, E., & Protheroe, N. (2000). Effective teaching: How do we know it when we see it? *The Informed Educator Series*. Arlington, VA: Educational Research Services.

Skrla, L. (2001). The influence of state accountability on teacher expectations and student performance. *UCEA: The Review, 42*(2), 1–4.

Skrla, L., Scheurich, J. J., & Johnson, J. F. (2000). *Equity-driven achievement-focused school districts*. Austin, TX: Charles A. Dana Center.

Smith, M. L. (1991). Put to the test: The effects of external testing on teachers. *Educational Researcher, 20*(5), 8–11.

Spring, J. (1990). *The American school 1642-1990* (2nd ed.). White Plains, NY: Longman.

Stake, R. (1999). The goods on American education. *Phi Delta Kappan, 80*, 668–672.

Stone, J. E. (1999). Value-added assessment: An accountability revolution. In M. Kanstoroom & C. E. Finn, Jr. (Eds.), *Better teachers, better schools*. Washington, DC: Thomas B. Fordham Foundation.

Strauss, R. P., & Sawyer, E. A. (1986). Some new evidence on teacher and student competencies. *Economics of Education Review, 5*(1), 41–48.

Stronge, J. H. (1997). Improving schools through teacher evaluation. In J. H. Stronge (Ed.), *Evaluating teaching: A guide to current thinking and best practice* (pp. 1–23). Thousand Oaks, CA: Corwin Press.

Stronge, J. H. (2002). *Qualities of effective teachers*. Alexandria, VA: Association for Supervision and Curriculum Development.

Stronge, J. H., & Tucker, P. D. (2000). *Teacher evaluation and student achievement*. Washington, DC: National Education Association.

Stronge, J. H., & Tucker, P. D. (2003). *Handbook on teacher evaluation: Assessing and improving performance*. Larchmont, NY: Eye on Education.

Stronge, J. H., Tucker, P. D., & Ward, T. J. (2003, April). *Teacher effectiveness and student learning: What do good teachers do?* Paper presented at the annual meeting of the American Educational Research Association, Chicago, IL.

Stufflebeam, D. L. (1997). Oregon Teacher Work Sample Methodology: Educational policy review. In J. Millman (Ed.), *Grading teachers, grading schools: Is student achievement a valid evaluation measure?* (pp. 53–61). Thousand Oaks, CA: Corwin Press.

Sykes, G. (1997). On trial: The Dallas value-added accountability system. In J. Millman (Ed.), *Grading teachers, grading schools: Is student achievement a valid evaluation measure?* Thousand Oaks, CA: Corwin Press.

Tennessee Department of Education. (2000). *Framework for Evaluation and Professional Development*. Nashville, TN: Office of Professional Development.

Thomas, J. A., & Montomery, P. (1998). On becoming a good teacher: Reflective practice with regard to children's voices. *Journal of Teacher Education, 49*(5), 372–380.

Thompson, J. G. (2002). *First-year teacher's survival kit*. San Francisco, CA: Jossey-Bass.

Thompson School District. (n.d.). *School professional evaluation: Toolkit for administrators and school professionals*. Loveland, CO: Author.

Thompson School District. (1996, August). *A parent's guide to standards*. Loveland, CO: Author.

Thompson School District. (1997–98). Teacher professional standards. *Thompson School District R2-J School Professional Evaluation Handbook*. Loveland, CO: Author.

Thum, Y. M., & Bryk, A. S. (1997). Value-added productivity indicators: The Dallas system. In J. Millman (Ed.), *Grading teachers, grading schools: Is student achievement a valid evaluation measure?* Thousand Oaks, CA: Corwin Press.

Tomlinson, C. A. (1999). *The differentiated classroom: Responding to the needs of all learners*. Alexandria, VA: Association for Supervision and Curriculum Development.

Tucker, P. D., & Stronge, J. H. (2001). Measure for measure: Using student test results in teacher evaluations. *American School Board Journal, 188*(9), 34–37.

Tyler, R. W. (1949). *Basic principles of curriculum and instruction*. Chicago: The University of Chicago Press.

University of Tennessee Value-Added Research and Assessment Center. (1997). *Graphical summary of educational findings from the Tennessee Value-Added Assessment System*. Knoxville, TN: Author.

Urban, W., & Wagoner, J. (2000). *American education: A history* (2nd Ed.). Boston: McGraw-Hill Higher Education.

Vaughan, A. C. (2002). Standards, accountability, and the determination of school success. *The Educational Forum, 22*, 206–213.

Viader, D., & Blair, J. (1999, September 29). Error affects test results in six states. *Education Week, 1*, 13–15.

Viadero, D. (2004, January 21). Achievement-gap study emphasizes better use of data. *Education Week*, p. 9.

Virginia Department of Education. (2003). Summary FY 2003: Increases in classroom teacher salaries. Retrieved February 25, 2004, from www.pen.k12.va.us/VDOE/Finance/Budget/2002-2003SalarySurvey-FinalRptforweb.pdf

Virginia State Department of Education. (2000). *Virginia school laws.* Charlottesville, VA: The Michie Company.

Walberg, H. J. (1984). Improving the productivity of America's schools. *Educational Leadership, 41*(8), 19–27.

Walberg, H. J., & Paik, S. J. (1997). Assessment requires incentives to add value: A review of the Tennessee Value-Added Assessment System. In J. Millman (Ed.), *Grading teachers, grading schools: Is student achievement a valid evaluation measure?* (pp. 169–178). Thousand Oaks, CA: Corwin Press.

Wang, M. C., Haertel, G. D., & Walberg, H. J. (1993). Toward a knowledge base for school learning. *Review of Educational Research, 63*(3), 249–294.

Wayne, A. J., & Youngs, P. (2003). Teacher characteristics and student achievement gains: A review. *Review of Educational Research, 73*(1), 89–122.

Wenglinsky, H. (2000). *How teaching matters: Bringing the classroom back into discussions of teacher quality.* Princeton, NJ: Millikan Family Foundation and Educational Testing Service.

Western Oregon University. (n.d.). *Teacher effectiveness project: The reliability and validity of Teacher Work Sample Methodology: A synopsis.* Monmouth, OR: Author.

Wharton-McDonald, R., Pressley, M., & Hampston, J. M. (1998). Literacy instruction in nine first-grade classrooms: Teacher characteristics and student achievement [Electronic version]. *The Elementary School Journal, 99*(2). Retrieved on October 30, 2003, from http://80-web3.infotrac.galegroup.com.proxy.wm.edu/itw/infomark/993/701/64058160w3/purl=rc1_EAIM_0_A54851458&dyn=4!ar_fmt?sw_aep=viva_wm

Wheeler, P. H. (1995). Before you use student tests in teacher evaluation . . . consider these issues. *AASPA Report.* Virginia Beach, VA: American Association of School Personnel Administrators.

Wiggins, G., & McTighe, J. (1998). *Understanding by design.* Alexandria, VA: Association for Supervision and Curriculum Development.

Wilkerson, D., Manatt, R., Rogers, M., & Maughan, R. (2000). Validation of student, principal, and self-ratings in 360-degree feedback for teacher evaluation. *Journal of Personnel Evaluation in Education, 14*(2), 179–192.

Wolf, K., Lichtenstein, G., & Stevenson, C. (1997). Portfolios in teacher evaluation. In J. H. Stronge (Ed.), *Evaluating teaching: A guide to current thinking and best practice* (pp. 193–214). Thousand Oaks, CA: Corwin Press.

Wolk, S. (2002). *Being good: Rethinking classroom management and student discipline.* Portsmouth, NH: Heinemann.

Wright, S. P., Horn, S. P., & Sanders, W. L. (1997). Teacher and classroom context effects on student achievement: Implications for teacher evaluation. *Journal of Personnel Evaluation in Education, 11,* 57–67.

Zahorik, J., Halbach, A., Ehrle, K., & Molnar, A. (2003). Teaching practices for smaller classes. *Educational Leadership, 61*(1), 75–77.

# Index

# About the Authors

**Pamela D. Tucker** is an associate professor of education in the Curry School of Education at the University of Virginia in Charlottesville, Virginia, where she serves as the director of the Principal Internship Program. Her research focuses on teacher effectiveness, the nature of the school principalship, and personnel evaluation. Books coauthored with others include: *Handbook for the Qualities of Effective Teachers* (Association for Supervision and Curriculum Development, 2004), *Handbook on Teacher Evaluation: Assessing and Improving Performance* and *Handbook on Educational Specialist Evaluation: Assessing and Improving Performance* (Eye on Education, 2003), *Educational Leadership in an Age of Accountability* (SUNY Press, 2003), *Teacher Evaluation and Student Achievement* (National Education Association, 2000), and *Handbook on Teacher Portfolios for Evaluation and Professional Development* (Eye on Education, 2000). Tucker's published articles address topics including teacher portfolios, helping struggling teachers, guidelines for linking student achievement and teacher evaluation, and the legal context for teacher evaluation. She has worked with numerous school districts and the

Commonwealth of Virginia in designing evaluation systems for teachers, administrators, and support personnel. She earned her doctorate in Educational Administration from the College of William and Mary, and has been a middle school teacher, special education teacher, and school administrator.

**James H. Stronge** is Heritage Professor in the Educational Policy, Planning, and Leadership Area at the College of William and Mary in Williamsburg, Virginia. Among his primary research interests are teacher effectiveness, student success, and teacher and administrator performance evaluation. He has worked with numerous school districts, state, and national educational organizations to design and develop evaluation systems for teachers, administrators, superintendents, and support personnel. He is the author, coauthor, or editor of numerous articles, books, and technical reports on teacher quality and performance evaluation, including the books *Handbook for the Qualities of Effective Teachers* (Association for Supervision and Curriculum Development, 2004), *Superintendent Evaluation Handbook* (Scarecrow Press, 2003), *Handbook on Teacher Evaluation* (Eye on Education, 2003), *Handbook on Educational Specialist Evaluation* (Eye on Education, 2003), *Qualities of Effective Teaching* (Association for Supervision and Curriculum Development, 2002), *Teacher Evaluation and Student Achievement* (National Education Association, 2000), *Handbook on Teacher Portfolios for Evaluation and Professional Development* (Eye-on-Education, 2000), *Evaluating Teaching: A Guide to Current Thinking and Best Practice* (Corwin Press, 1997), and *Evaluating Professional Support Personnel in Education* (Sage Publications, 1991). He received his doctorate in Educational Administration and Planning from the University of Alabama. He has been a teacher, counselor, and district-level administrator.

**Melissa McBride** is a doctoral student in the Administration and Supervision program in the Curry School of Education at the University of Virginia in Charlottesville, Virginia. Her research interests include teacher effectiveness, teacher and administrator preparation, and diversity issues in education. Prior to her doctoral studies, McBride was a special education teacher, basketball and tennis coach, and a high school administrator. She is a trained multicultural education facilitator and has led staff development sessions and presented on various topics regarding equity and diversity. McBride is currently the field supervisor of the Administrative Internship Program. As part of the Carnegie Foundation's *Teachers for a New Era* grant, she is assisting university faculty in a research study of teacher preparation in Virginia. McBride's professional aspirations include working as a secondary school principal and special education consultant. She holds a bachelor of science in Special Education from The College of New Jersey (formerly Trenton State College) and a masters of education degree in Administration and Supervision from the University of Virginia.

**Mason Miller** is a doctoral student in the Administration and Supervision program in the Curry School of Education at the University of Virginia in Charlottesville, Virginia. His research interests are focused on school leadership preparation and teacher evaluation. Prior to graduate study, he taught middle and high school English in Wyoming, California, and Virginia. Miller served in various leadership capacities during his teaching career, including school site council chair, district-level curriculum committee member, and 8th grade team leader. He has worked with University of Virginia faculty on a number of projects, most recently taking part in the design, dissemination, and analysis of a survey examining alumni perceptions of the school leadership preparation experience. In the near future, Miller plans to become a secondary school principal and work with aspiring school administrators at the university level. He holds degrees from Case Western Reserve University and Boston College.

## Related ASCD Resources
## Linking Teacher Evaluation and Student Achievement

At the time of publication, the following ASCD resources were available; for the most up-to-date information about ASCD resources, go to www.ascd.org. ASCD stock numbers are noted in parentheses.

### Mixed Media

*Analyzing Teaching: A Professional Development* (2 CD-ROMs) (#503367)

*Making School Improvement Happen with What Works in Schools: Teacher Level Factors,* Action Tool (#NEED STOCK NUMBER)

### Networks

Visit the ASCD Web site (www.ascd.org) and search for "networks" for information about professional educators who have formed groups around topics like "Mentoring Leadership and Resources." Look in the "Network Directory" for current facilitators' addresses and phone numbers.

### Online Resources

Visit ASCD's Web site (www.ascd.org) for the following professional development opportunities:

Professional Development Online: *Exemplary Assessment: Measurement That's Useful and Teacher Behaviors That Promote Assessment for Learning,* among others (for a small fee; password protected)

### Print Products

*Collaborative Analysis of Student Work: Improving Teaching and Learning* by Georgea M. Langer, Amy B. Colton, and Loretta S. Goff (#102006)

*Educational Leadership: Evaluating Educators* (entire issue, February 2001) Excerpted articles online free; entire issue online and accessible to ASCD members (#101034)

*Enhancing Professional Practice: A Framework for Teaching* by Charlotte Danielson (#196074)

*Handbook for Qualities of Effective Teachers* by James H. Stronge, Pamela D. Tucker, and Jennifer L. Hindman (#104135)

*Qualities of Effective Teachers* by James H. Stronge (#102007)

*Teacher Evaluation to Enhance Professional Practice* by Charlotte Danielson and Thomas McGreal (copublished with the Educational Testing Service) (#100219)

*Teaching What Matters Most: Standards and Strategies for Raising Student Achievement* by Richard W. Strong, Harvey F. Silver, and Matthew J. Perini (#100057)

*The Truth About Testing: An Educator's Call to Action* by W. John Popham (#101030)

### DVD and Video

*Mentoring the New Teacher: Evaluating Student Work* (#494013)

*Qualities of Effective Teachers* (with facilitator's guide) (#604423 DVD; #404423 VHS; #704423 bundle)

*A Visit to Classrooms of Effective Teachers* (#NEED STOCK NUMBERS FOR DVD AND VHS)

For more information, visit us on the World Wide Web (http://www.ascd.org), send an e-mail message to member@ascd.org, call the ASCD Service Center (1-800-933-ASCD or 703-578-9600, then press 2), send a fax to 703-575-5400, or write to Information Services, ASCD, 1703 N. Beauregard St., Alexandria, VA 22311-1714 USA.